AGAINST
THE ODDS

THE ADVENTURES OF A MAN IN HIS SIXTIES COMPETING IN SIX OF
THE WORLD'S TOUGHEST TRIATHLONS ACROSS SIX CONTINENTS

1165

John Pendergrass

AGAINST
THE ODDS

hatherleigh

⫸ hatherleigh

Hatherleigh Press is committed to preserving and protecting the natural resources of the earth. Environmentally responsible and sustainable practices are embraced within the company's mission statement.

Visit us at www.hatherleighpress.com and register online for free offers, discounts, special events, and more.

Cover Design by Carolyn Kasper / DCDesigns
Interior Design by Carolyn Kasper / DCDesigns

Printed in the United States

10 9 8 7 6 5 4 3 2 1

IRONMAN and 70.3 are registered trademarks of World Triathlon Corporation.

www.hatherleighpress.com

DEDICATION

Polly, John, Eric, and Patricia

PROLOGUE

THIS IS not a serious book. There are no deeper meanings or hidden revelations buried in its pages. Everything really did happen just as I described, but I've changed a few names to avoid embarrassing anyone.

I'm making the standard disclaimer that all mistakes belong to me. Hopefully they are few and far between.

As much as possible I've avoided the metric system, even though it's standard for international competition and for much of the rest of the world.

CONTENTS

PROLOGUE   vii

FOREWORD   by Brett Favre   xi

CHAPTER 1   China on My Mind   1

CHAPTER 2   Looking for a Challenge   13

CHAPTER 3   "Whoever Finishes First, We'll Call
            Him the IRONMAN'"   17

CHAPTER 4   Triathlon 101   23

CHAPTER 5   The IRONMAN® Mystique   33

CHAPTER 6   In the Pool and On the Road   41

CHAPTER 7   Adventures in South America: Brazil   59

CHAPTER 8   No Country for an Old Man: Switzerland   87

CHAPTER 9   Hurricanes and Hip Fractures   109

CHAPTER 10   Back on the Road: South Africa   125

CHAPTER 11   A Land of Great Surprises: New Zealand   143

CHAPTER 12   A Crowd in the Desert: Arizona   165

CHAPTER 13   The Sixth and Final Stop: China   179

EPILOGUE   199

ACKNOWLEDGMENTS   201

FOREWORD

I'M NO expert on triathlons, though my wife has been a triathlete for the last several years. Running I understand—I've done a fair bit of it throughout my 20 years in the NFL—but once you add swimming and biking into the mix, the whole thing starts to look a lot more daunting. Then you figure out how long the distances are—about 2,500 football fields worth—and you start to understand why the title of "IRONMAN®" is so coveted, and why the finishers are so respected.

What I *am* an expert at is going to work every day, doing your best, and never giving up. I know all about playing hard and having fun. I also know about devoting all of my time, energy, and passion to a sport whose challenges are their own rewards. And I know about the overwhelming feeling of accomplishment that comes from achieving something that everyone told you was impossible.

I have been fortunate enough to enjoy one of the longest careers in the NFL and have experienced first-hand how it feels to grow older with your sport. I'm living proof that preconceptions about what a man is capable of based on his age aren't worth the paper they're printed on.

Reading *Against the Odds*, I found something in John Pendergrass that I could identify with. When I wrestled with one of the hardest decisions of my life—whether or not to leave a sport that I've dedicated my life to—there were so many people who felt the need to add their two cents. People told me that it was time for me to step aside, that retirement was the only option. And I know that John must have heard the same judgments, offered in the same tone from his family and friends about why he should give up on his goals.

The phrase, "you're only as old as you feel," is tossed around a lot, usually by people who are starting to feel older than they'd like. But this is actually very true. It's a truth that both John and I have learned from our own experiences. At age 60, when most people spend their leisure time riding in a golf cart or sitting in front of a television, John Pendergrass chose to hit the road, traveling to six continents and competing in six IRONMAN® Triathlons. He has collected enough aches and pains and racked up enough frequent flyer miles for a man half his age.

Against the Odds is a remarkable story, a tale of courage and perseverance told with humor and honesty. There must be thousands of athletes who have finished an IRONMAN race faster than John Pendergrass, but there can't be very many who have had as interesting a journey.

— BRETT FAVRE

CHINA

NORTH
VIETNAM
HANOI

LAOS

HAIKOU
HAINAN

SOUTH
CHINA SEA

DA NANG

SOUTH
VIETNAM

CAMBODIA

HO CHI MINH CITY
(SAIGON)

SOUTHEAST ASIA

Chapter 1

CHINA ON MY MIND

HAIKOU, CHINA, has to be one of the hottest places on earth. It's early March, a time when much of the world is still slumbering through winter, eagerly anticipating the coming days of spring. Here, at the bottom of China, things seem to have skipped into summer. It's already in the nineties, and each day is a little warmer than the day before.

I'm in town for the 2010 IRONMAN® China, an endurance event that packs a month's worth of swimming, biking, and running into a single nonstop day. It starts at the break of dawn with a 2.4 mile open-water swim, continues through the day with a 112 mile bike and finishes with a 26.2 mile run. An IRONMAN Triathlon is a physical and mental challenge unlike anything else in the world, the culmination of months of training and preparation.

Haikou is the capital of Hainan, an island province nestled in the tropical South China Sea at the southern tip of mainland China. Not many people travel this far to do an IRONMAN race, but for me it's another opportunity to get a little off the beaten path and try something different and difficult in a distant land.

This is my sixth IRONMAN® Triathlon and each one has been on a different continent. There may be a few other people who have done this, but there can't be many. The travel and training take their toll. IRON-MAN Triathlons have a way of dominating your life, destroying your free time, whittling down your bank account. It's a sport that seems to invite and reward obsession, but even the obsessed can grow weary and exhausted. Still, some people hang on longer than others. In my travels I've run across athletes who seem to have dedicated their entire life to the IRONMAN ethic. They show a frightening single-mindedness. Their families and jobs fade into the background as they train like demons, pounding out the miles, seemingly oblivious to pain and suffering.

These folks all have a few things in common. They're all younger than I am, stronger than I am, smarter than I am. I'm a late-starter, out of place and over my head in a young man's game.

At age sixty, when most men are looking at their IRA, hoping that it's going up, and checking their PSA, hoping that it's staying down, I started doing IRONMAN Triathlons.

I'm probably the first person in his sixties to ever try six IRONMAN Triathlons on six continents, but who knows? When you're old, the times are slow and the records are sparse. At my age, the rewards come in the form of indelible memories rather than record performances. Six decades is a long time, it's a time of life when many people disappear. I'm happy to have made it this far, glad to still be moving about in the land of the living.

The Chinese agree: they consider me a fortunate man. Six is a lucky number in China, a symbol of good fortune and smooth sailing. Six IRONMAN Triathlons, six continents, all in my sixties—666. I've got one of the luckiest numbers in the Middle Kingdom. The Chinese seem to infuse these sixes with a spiritual meaning, they see me as one of the chosen few.

Brazil, Switzerland, South Africa, New Zealand, Arizona—I've got plenty of time to reflect back on my previous IRONMAN® races. Most of my free moments here in China have been spent lying in my hotel room, soaking in sweat, wishing the air conditioner worked better. It's a toasty 80 degrees in my room, maybe the Chinese don't mind the heat or maybe the good AC units have all been shipped back home to Walmart.

I've got an intractable case of jet lag and I'm forced to spend many of my bonus waking hours hovering near the toilet, hoping my gastro-intestinal problems work themselves out by race day. Sometimes when I finally manage to doze off, the pain in my right shoulder awakens me and reminds me that my rotator cuff has seen its better days.

My list of grievances seems to be self-replenishing. If one problem gets a little better, a new one pops up to take its place. Lesser complaints become major calamities as new troubles move to the front.

This trip to China seems to be the exception in my IRONMAN journeys; usually I'm a good traveler. I enjoy meeting new people, seeing places I've read about for years, eating different foods. I try to take my time, reduce my expectations, and make it a point not to get upset if things turn out differently than I had hoped. Jet lag is always there, but normally it disappears by the second day. I eat simply for a couple of days before the race, stay away from uncooked food, and drink plenty of bottled fluids. By race morning I'm usually feeling good, raring to get started, and anxious to get done. I never have a problem cranking up the energy and optimism.

This trip is different. China has a special set of problems.

I'm staying at a resort hotel fronting on the South China Sea, some five miles or so outside of town. It's not a bad spot; they charge me more for one night than a local peasant makes in a couple of months. Like most places in China, the tap water isn't drinkable so I have to boil it in my cof-feepot. There's a small refrigerator in my room that must have been built at the same factory that made the air conditioning unit. It hums loudly and drowns out the television, but it doesn't cool. Here at the resort, I am part of a captive audience. When I eat or drink at the hotel or visit the gift shop, I pay rates that would make Donald Trump blush.

There are some good points, though. The hotel employees are very friendly. They like to practice their English and it gives me the opportunity to try out the few Chinese phrases I've learned. I think my Southern drawl throws them for a loop; it's a far cry from the elegant British accent heard on the BBC. Plus, it's nice to see that each day the end of the roll of toilet paper in my room is folded into a perfect triangle. That's something that never happens at home.

Besides, I always try to stay positive. You never know; fortune can come in odd disguises. Some days I lie in bed and watch a Chinese docudrama about Chairman Mao (it is on TV every day). I smile, toast the Great Helmsman with a large glass of freshly boiled water, and prepare for my own upcoming Long March.

On other days, when my body cooperates, I ride from the hotel into town, passing peasants in straw hats stooped and working in the rice fields. It's a glimpse back in time, a look at agricultural techniques that probably haven't changed for centuries. The nation of China is a strange mixture. Certain parts of the country have the feel of a place that has only been built recently, while other parts seem to date from the time of Confucius. The very old and the very new are side by side.

Many of the Chinese fill the roads on bicycles, scooters, pedicycles, broken-down carts, old trucks—anything on wheels is placed into action. The traffic in China is wild and woolly, a game of vehicular pinball. Automobiles are relatively new to the country. As one observer noted, the Chinese appear to have learned how to drive by watching *The Dukes of Hazzard.*

Downtown Haikou is an almost impenetrable mass of people, crowds swarming at every angle. Everyone seems to be in continuous motion, chattering, bumping, staring, rarely stopping for more than a moment. There's no concept of personal space in China. No one ever queues; if someone needs your spot, stand erect, steady your legs, and be prepared to push back.

This vast number of human souls, this great swarm of mankind, is what strikes everyone who comes to China. Getting around is sometimes exhausting, often bewildering, always exciting.

Haikou is closing in on a population of two million. China itself officially has 1.3 billion people, a fifth of the world's population. Some think the real number is closer to a billion and a half. There are at least 90 cities in the country with a population of a million or more (by contrast, there are only nine in the United States). Many of the places are easily recognizable—Beijing, Shanghai, Chongqing, Hong Kong, but there are dozens with names that I've never heard of and couldn't begin to pronounce, places like Zibo, Qiqihar, and Yantai.

The streets of Haikou are a wonderland of the strange and exotic. The food stalls and small restaurants are filled with every type of produce known to man. Huge bags of tea, unrecognizable carcasses of unknown animals, large sacks of spices, strange-looking creatures from the sea, common weeds and grasses, bubbling pots of Lord knows what.

In China when it comes to food, anything goes and nothing is wasted. Chicken heads, or penises, pigeon brains, cow's lung, they're all there to sample if the mood strikes you.

For a man with an unstable gastrointestinal tract, this is an olfactory overload, I need to tread lightly. Wisely, I decide to avoid the grilled dog meat, and look for a Pizza Hut instead.

Things may seem a little strange here in China, but who am I to complain. The Chinese consider me, like most foreigners, to be a loathsome barbarian, a heathen out of place in their great civilized country.

Besides, one man's scorpion is another man's sirloin steak.

■ ■ ■

A few months ago this China trip sounded like a great idea. I had just returned from a race in Arizona and I was anxious to do my sixth and final IRONMAN race. IRONMAN China would be my fourth IRONMAN Triathlon in less than two years. It seemed as if I was in a constant training mode leading up to the IRONMAN race, I was spending more time with my bicycle than with my wife, and I constantly reeked of chlorine. My running shoes were becoming as worn, stretched, and beaten as my body. When I first got out of bed in the morning, my muscles and joints were stiff and immobile, almost petrified. My body felt like it had been beaten and left for dead; it was ready for the funeral home. I knew that I needed a break, but I hoped to squeeze in one final race and complete my six-continent journey.

Stacking IRONMAN races in close succession is never a good choice at any age, but for me, I knew the clock was ticking fast. I wasn't concerned about being the first old guy to try six continents, I simply knew that my days running IRONMAN races were numbered. I had gotten old and time had taken its toll. I'm on the weak side of sixty. It's a decade of life when your body betrays you day by day. Simple tasks become complex, easy things become difficult. You're never in as good a shape as you were last year, what you lose you never get back.

If my body was a checking account, it would have to be marked "Overdrawn: Insufficient Funds."

■ ■ ■

Even though I was living close to the edge and courting disaster, I really wanted to go to China. Nostalgia never goes out of style for someone in their sixties and my Chinese trip had turned into an Oriental version of *You Can't Go Home Again*, an opportunity to go four decades into the past and rediscover wartime experiences.

I'm headed to Hainan Island for the 2010 IRONMAN China. Forty years ago, Hainan was a place I did my damnedest to stay away from.

Back then if I had somehow wandered too far into the Far East I would have ended up as a permanent guest of the People's Republic of China.

In those distant days, when Richard Nixon was President, I was serving as a flight surgeon in the U.S. Air Force. This was during the Vietnam War and my choice assignment was Da Nang Air Base in South Vietnam, barely a hundred and fifty miles southwest of Hainan. Most of my friends and classmates managed to skip the Vietnam conflict but I was a little slow in figuring things out. I looked up one day and there I was in Southeast Asia, as far away from Mississippi as a poor man can get.

My unit, the 366th Tactical Fighter Wing, was one of the USAF's most decorated fighter wings with a record of service extending from World War II to the present time. Known as the "Gunfighters," the 366th was one of the first fighter wings to be sent to Vietnam and was the very last one to leave.

The Vietnam conflict, like all wars, had enough absurdity and tragedy to last a lifetime, but it had its exciting moments, too. During my tour in Vietnam, I lived with my fighter squadron and spent most of my time looking out for their health and safety, but I also logged 54 combat missions in the back seat of an F-4 Phantom. The Phantom was the workhorse fighter of the Vietnam War, a supersonic machine, full of thunder and thrust that practically exploded off the runway. It was the fastest thing in a fast-moving world, perfect for someone like me, very impressionable and too young to know better.

In the back seat of an F-4, I was the navigator, radio operator, and weapons man, plus I got a lot of informal flying time. In Air Force parlance I was a GIB (Guy in the Backseat), a vital member of the two-man air crew. The other pilots and navigators were brave and fearless, but I was more of a curious coward, afraid of missing something exciting, anxious not to be left out.

I was a budding navigator, and all navigators love maps. The island of Hainan sat like a lump of coal in the upper right-hand corner of my charts. It was worse than Hanoi, more dangerous than Haiphong. It might as well have been labeled "Hell." Everyone knew that Hainan was a place to avoid at all costs. Invading Chinese airspace was never a part of any of our flight plans.

Most of the combat missions I flew during my tour were in Laos, a part of the never-ending battle to keep men and material from coming from North Vietnam via the Ho Chi Minh trail into South Vietnam. Some of our flights went to North Vietnam, and there the risks escalated greatly. The North was the worst place of all to fly. Anti-aircraft fire (AAA) went from a possibility to a near certainty. Flying up north was like winning a chance to play Russian roulette, an opportunity to at best break even. Since it was a disaster waiting to happen, a quick in and out of the country was always the safest choice. Hainan and the Chinese MIGs loomed just over the horizon, only a few minutes away. It doesn't take long to cover 50 to 100 miles in a Mach 2 fighter.

Unless of course you're heading back from a mission; then it seems to takes an eternity.

■ ■ ■

For me, the flights in South Vietnam and Laos were bad, but the missions over North Vietnam were terrifying. The evenings before I was scheduled to fly over North Vietnam were in many ways very similar to the evenings before I competed in an IRONMAN® Triathlon. It was the same style emotional roller coaster, a time to question your courage, your competence, your sanity.

In both cases I would lie in bed wondering, "What the hell am I doing?" From a distance these physically difficult and dangerous challenges had a definite appeal. It was my opportunity to rise to the occasion, to do things that few people had ever done, to join an exclusive club, to go a step further than necessary. It's always easy to be adventurous and fearless from afar. I've always had great armchair courage, it's probably more of a curse than a blessing.

As the day of reckoning got closer, the fear and apprehension would bubble to the surface. I would get the feeling that I had really gone and done it this time, I had overstepped, screwed up royally, and now I was getting ready to pay a big price for my foolish bravado.

Next would come an even bigger barrage of self-criticism. I knew that I didn't have to fly over North Vietnam, I didn't even have to fly a combat mission. I could have safely earned my flight pay bouncing around on a transport plane (what the fighter jocks derisively called "trash haulers") instead of flying over the most dangerous place on earth.

There are some similar emotions for an IRONMAN® event. Why did I sign up for this crazy race? I could have done any short triathlon, no one knows the difference. Who says you have to compete, anyway? Why did I pay good money to do something so stupid?

Eventually I would realize that all the self-criticism was pointless. Even though I had beaten myself to a pulp, I knew that there was no escaping, my time was coming in the morning. I would pass the evening sleeping fitfully, mostly lying in bed and brooding, an unpleasant mixture of anxiety, self-pity, and despair.

On the eve of the battle, voluntarily taking on the great challenge makes no sense at all. There's only self-doubt, loneliness, and hopelessness. I wonder what happened to my brain, what was I thinking?

■ ■ ■

The reward, of course, comes at the finish.

After a mission over North Vietnam, the trip from the flight line to the debriefing room is one of the best walks you'll ever have in your life. If I had encountered anti-aircraft fire it was even better. Everyone in my squadron soon learned about it. The news was included in the intelligence briefing for upcoming flights and became a part of the flight line gossip. "Hey, Doc, those Viet Cong are after your ass," someone would say, "you'd better watch it." "I wasn't worried," I'd reply; surely one of the biggest lies I've ever told in my entire life. Just a few hours before I had sworn to myself that I would never fly another combat mission, now I was looking forward to the next time out.

After an IRONMAN® Triathlon, it's a little bit of the same thing; a feeling of pride and relief, mission accomplished. Your heart rate is back to normal (it goes up in both cases for different reasons) and you start thinking about your next race. You can forget pain just like you can forget danger; it's easy to airbrush away the bad memories. The accomplishments never go away; they can be revisited many times.

These are rich emotions; you've moved a little closer to the edge without getting burned. You've pushed your luck in a place you don't belong and gotten away with it. You persevered in hard times, looking for that one crowded hour of life.

Of course, not everyone sees life this way. It's hard to describe the joys of the slightly irrational. Sometimes I try to explain all of this to my wife. She probably thinks I'm crazy. I'm not sure how she really feels; she seems to vacillate between admiration and resignation.

■ ■ ■

Modern life and the good old days are coming together nicely. The more I think about my return to Southeast Asia for the IRONMAN race, the better the project sounds. I was stationed in Vietnam in those antediluvian times before the sport of triathlon had been invented. In those days, there was no such thing as an IRONMAN Triathlon. Fancy bicycles and expensive running shoes were still years away, Schwinn and Converse® were the brands of the time. When you got thirsty you drank water, not a sports drink. When you got tired you didn't reach for an energy gel, you just pushed a little harder to get to the end. It was 1974, long after Vietnam, before someone thought to put swimming, biking, and running together in one continuous competition.

Back in those Vietnam days, biking was an activity for kids or for those effete Europeans or, at best, back up transportation for poor Americans who couldn't afford a car. Swimming was something the youngsters did in summer, except every four years when it showed up at the Olympics.

Forty years is a long time, but the whole idea sounds more impressive to me as each day passes. Time does a lot of things. It marches on, it heals all wounds, it stops for no man, and it can even fly when you're having fun. One thing time doesn't do is soften my enthusiasm or dampen my accomplishments. In my mind, this IRONMAN® trip is getting bigger every day.

Chapter 2

LOOKING FOR A
CHALLENGE

THIS WHOLE IRONMAN® project happened on its own.
There was no grand strategy, no master plan. I've always been
reluctant to go too far into the future; there's enough happening
in the present to keep me occupied. I never thought of traveling
around the world, bouncing from continent to continent, carrying a bicycle the way most people carry a suitcase, knocking off
an IRONMAN Triathlon at each port of call. That was much too
grandiose an idea, too pretentious to even contemplate.

Instead, like most of my life, I simply followed along as one
thing led to another, more like a passenger on life's train than the
engineer. Small challenges begat bigger challenges, short journeys
became longer journeys, friends and family grew accustomed to
seeing me leave town, my partners learned to no longer count on

me for any meaningful work. These trips began to seem second nature, the preparations became routine, one race led to the next. It all seemed pre-ordained.

The IRONMAN® adventure started the year I turned 60.

At that time, my life was rolling along smoothly, almost on cruise control. My three children were out of college and off the payroll. There was no mortgage on the home, my office building was paid in full. I had a more manageable schedule in my medical practice with less night work and more free weekends.

As the new decade approached, I noticed how things were changing. Store clerks all addressed me as "Sir." The folks at the AARP wrote me regularly. I could see Medicare and Social Security just over the horizon waiting to welcome me into the Golden Age, the life of fulsome leisure. My children no longer saw me as a dictator, instead I was more of an enlightened monarch. The large bumps on the road of life had disappeared for the time being. I knew that the nursing home might be just a few years away, but it was time for a new challenge. This was the 19th hole of life and I needed something big to shoot for, something to stoke the fire in this decrepit, dormant body of mine.

There were a lot of new experiences I could have tried. I could have worked on my golf game or maybe concentrated on becoming a better fisherman or perhaps enlisted in the church softball league. By and large, these things consist of large blocks of idle time with just a few micro-moments of real action. At my age I need more bang for the buck in everything I do. I needed to do something that just a few people have done, something that bordered on the impossible, something that would require a big time commitment. In other words, a great challenge for a less than great body.

Marathons, bicycle century rides, trail runs, they're all tough, but I decided to aim even higher. Why not shoot for an IRONMAN Triathlon, the most difficult one-day endurance event in the world?

I thought it over. At age sixty, it required a bit of an irrational leap of faith but from my easy chair it looked very doable, and after a few beers, I knew I was up to the task.

■ ■ ■

Triathlons have been around for a while and the IRONMAN® Triathlon is the most iconic of them all. The IRONMAN World Championship is held each fall in Hawaii and most people have at least seen bits of the competition on television. The IRONMAN name conveys strength, endurance, determination, perseverance—all virtues that I feared I was lacking. My body was flabby and saggy and my willpower was weak, but I knew that it would be now or never. Time waits for no man.

I didn't embrace the IRONMAN idea outright. I sort of nibbled at the edges. Over the years I've run some marathons and in the last few years I've done several triathlons.

Since the concepts of time and distance are vaguely familiar to me, I knew I might be biting off too much. I broke the IRONMAN idea gradually to my wife, Polly. After more than 35 years of marriage, I've learned how to introduce new ideas. I'm nothing if not clever and subtle.

"I'm thinking of doing an IRONMAN Triathlon," I say one morning over coffee.

"That's nice," she replies. "You've done those before, haven't you?" My wife is an intelligent woman in good physical shape. She's a great walker, covering several miles a day. However, race details and distances are a little foggy for her. Marathons, fun runs, triathlons, duathlons, 5 kilometer runs—they're all one big blur to her.

"No, I've done some triathlons before," I say, "but I've never done an IRONMAN Triathlon."

"Is that the one in Hawaii?" she asks.

"That's the main one," I reply, "but they have them all over the world."

"How far is the race?" she inquires.

"The swim is 2.4 miles in open water, a lake or ocean," I tell her. "Then there's a 112 mile bike followed by a full marathon, 26.2 miles."

"Good Lord, how long does it take you to do all that?" she asks.

"The race starts at 7:00 a.m. and ends at midnight," I reply. "I've got to finish in 17 hours or less or it doesn't count."

"Are you sure you're not too old for all that?" she asks. "You complain about how hard it is to take out the garbage. Every time you cut the grass you need a couple of beers to recover. You know you'll be 60 in a few months."

Uncertainty hovers, maybe she's right. Things don't move like they used to and getting out of bed in the morning takes a little longer. The other night while watching television I got stuck in my recliner chair. Maybe my day has come and gone.

Then, with a reassuring smile, she looks at me and says, "I know you'll do well."

Chapter 3

"WHOEVER FINISHES FIRST, WE'LL CALL HIM THE IRONMAN®"

I F THE sporting world was like the stock market, triathlon would be the great new growth stock for the modern era. Much like Google, Facebook, or some other high tech company, the sport has seemingly emerged from nowhere to become a widely recognized part of today's culture. A few decades ago no one had heard of triathlon. Now most everyone has done a triathlon, wants to do a triathlon, or knows someone who has done a triathlon. Triathlon started slow and grew modestly for years before coming of age in the twenty-first century.

It's a young sport. The modern version of swim, bike, and run only began in 1974. Like a lot of modern trends, both good and bad, triathlon started in the land of milk and honey, the great state of California, before spreading to the rest of the country.

Today, the principal governing body for the sport in our country is USA Triathlon (USAT), an organization responsible for selecting and training the elite athletes that represent the United States in the Olympic Games, the Pan Am Games, and the World Championship. Just as important, USAT also sanctions the many hundreds of triathlons held each year in this country, events ranging from short sprint triathlons all the way up to the full competition.

The distances of the various triathlons vary. There are long ones and short ones, hard ones and tough ones, but they all have a common thread: swim followed by bike followed by run.

In 1978, a group of endurance athletes living in Hawaii debated the merits of their particular sport. Is running a marathon harder than a 100 mile bike race? What about open water swimming with miles of big waves and strong currents? Who are the most fit—runners, cyclists, or swimmers?

U.S. Navy Commander John Collins knew how to settle that question. Rather than argue about which is the most difficult event, he decided to do all three. Collins combined the three long-distance competitions held annually on the island of Oahu—the Waikiki Roughwater Swim (2.4 miles), the Around Oahu Bike Race (115 miles), and the Honolulu Marathon (26.2 miles). The races would be run in succession on one day, Collins decreed. He tweaked the bike course, reducing it from 115 miles to 112 miles for logistical reasons, but the swim and run were left unchanged.

Three events, no breaks. The clock starts at the beginning of the swim and stops 140.6 miles later when you cross the finish line of the run. This is an IRONMAN® Triathlon.

What a punishing mixture of events. Mile on top of mile, hour after hour, no respite from the moving clock. An IRONMAN Triathlon is cruel by design, a race without symmetry or logic. Many thousands of future athletes would have Collins to thank for creating one of the most daunting physical challenges of all time.

Fifteen madmen started the 1978 race, and each received the now famous charge, "Swim 2.4 miles. Bike 112 miles. Run 26.2 miles. Brag for the rest of your life." Collins proceeded to coin one of the most iconic names for a sporting event: "Whoever finishes first, we'll call him the IRONMAN®." What a great choice. What a stroke of genius. IRONMAN athlete, the name says it all. The IRONMAN Triathlon was destined to become the world's premier multi-sport event, a brand that will eventually rival the Super Bowl®, the Masters, the Kentucky Derby. Collins surely had no idea of what he had created.

Most of the credit for the boom in today's IRONMAN race goes to Dr. James P. Gills and World Triathlon Corporation (WTC). In 1990, Dr. Gills, a well-known Florida ophthalmologist and an accomplished endurance athlete, bought the IRONMAN branded series of triathlon races and formed WTC. Since then, everything about IRONMAN racing has gotten bigger and better.

Looking back, the men of 1978 were the founding fathers; they were present at the creation, the first of many thousands to nearly kill themselves for no logical reason. For special occasions like the 25th anniversary of the first IRONMAN race, these athletes return to Hawaii for recognition. It's sort of like Old-Timers' Day at Yankee Stadium, but without the pinstripes. Today, these guys are older, they stoop a little, they are a little heavier, and their hair is thinner. They suffer from a variety of ailments, but that's okay. These are men I can identify with, they look just like me.

■ ■ ■

Like many people, I've been watching parts of these televised IRON-MAN events for years and the special stories from the competitors are very moving. The courage and tenacity of these athletes are amazing and inspiring. Those who succeed are overcome with joy, it's an elixir of euphoria. Those who fail, and there are always some, are crushed. Their disappointment and despair are so real, so deep. IRONMAN® racing is drama and suspense piled on top of sublime pathos.

Probably the most memorable event in all of IRONMAN history happened at the 1982 IRONMAN World Championship. It was an historic finish shown repeatedly on Wide World of Sports and picked up by many regular news outlets. If your brain has room for just one IRONMAN memory, this is probably the one.

Viewers of the day watched as Julie Moss, a 23-year-old former college student headed toward the finish line about to win the 1982 IRONMAN World Championship. She was tall, thin, and dressed in blue and white shorts and singlet with a funny-looking trucker cap anchored over her blond hair. Moss appeared to be moving along nicely but then, unexpectedly, as she approached the finish line, she began to weave and stagger. She fell on the ground, turned on her back, and then regained her feet. Race officials clustered around her, looking uncomfortable, confused. When someone collapses, the normal reaction is to come to the rescue. The officials wanted to help but may have been unaware of what they were permitted to do.

Moss stumbled and fell again, probably no more than 30 yards from the finish line and victory. There was a growing crowd around her, encouraging her, doing anything legal to help. Several male competitors ran by headed to the finish, and then on the periphery of the crowd, another female runner flashed by. Katherine McCartney passed Moss in the final yards to win the IRONMAN title.

Moss didn't quit, though. She was on her hands and knees crawling like a toddler toward the elusive finish line. Not just a few feet, but 5, 10, 15 or more yards. At last, she collapsed on her back astride the finish line.

Here is an athlete, crawling like a baby, totally exhausted, unable to walk, determined to finish no matter what the cost. The impression is dramatic and durable. An IRONMAN Triathlon isn't just physical, it's spiritual. It challenges the body and soul.

. . .

So how can I earn the glory that comes from being an IRONMAN® finisher? Where do I go to put my name on the list?

The IRONMAN triathlon in Kailua-Kona, Hawaii is the original IRONMAN race and also serves as the IRONMAN World Championship. In most cases you must qualify for the IRONMAN World Championship at another IRONMAN race, so that's out for me. I'm going to be doing my very first one.

There are another thirty or so IRONMAN races held around the world. These events are the same distance as the race in Hawaii and they are open to anyone willing to ante up the entry fee (some $500 or so and headed much higher) and sign away all their free time for four to six months.

But my choices are limited. Because of the logistics involved, each race handles a maximum of around 2,500 athletes. The events in the United States are very popular and sell out quickly. Normally registration for the following year begins online the day after the race concludes. Usually it takes less than a day for the race to fill.

Fortunately, the races in foreign countries don't sell out so quickly.

No one has called and invited me to Hawaii. I'd better start looking for my own IRONMAN race.

Chapter 4

TRIATHLON 101

BEFORE HEADING to IRONMAN® country, I need to be sure I've got this triathlon business down cold. I've done a few short races, but I need to learn all the ins and outs of how triathlons work.

I start hanging around with the Big Guys, the triathlon veterans, and I start asking probing, intelligent questions, like, "What do you do when you feel like you're drowning?" "Is it okay to stop pedaling so you can catch your breath?" "Should you be worried when you have chest pain every time you run?"

Everyone tells me that the rules of the triathlon world are sharp and simple. If I pay attention to what they say, there's no way I can get lost. I listen carefully.

Pretty soon everything is clear as a bell.

■ ■ ■

Today's triathlons come in a variety of distances. The most common by far is the sprint triathlon. There are hundreds of these races staged in communities all around the country. If it's warm enough to bike and swim, there's probably a sprint triathlon close by.

The exact race distance varies—a half mile swim, 15 to 20 mile bike and three mile run might be typical—but some races are a little longer and some are a little shorter. Often the distance depends on what roads are available for use by the race organizer. A 15 mile bike course might be easy to lay out and block off, while a 20 mile route would be impossible. The logistics of hosting a triathlon are much more difficult than those of staging a running event.

A sprint triathlon is a real challenge, but it's within the reach of most people. If you run regularly, you can add a few outings on the bike and some time in the pool and consider yourself in training for a sprint triathlon. It's a reasonable goal for reasonable people.

Practically everyone starts with a sprint triathlon before progressing to a longer event and many of the sprint triathlons have a beginners' division to encourage new participants. There are plenty of opportunities to compete in these shorter races and, before you know it, you're hooked on triathlons. Once you've done a sprint triathlon, it's natural to begin thinking of a longer event. For most of us, life's accomplishments come in short steps and small bites.

The next step up is an Olympic distance triathlon, a standard 0.93 mile swim, 24.8 mile bike, and 6.2 mile run. A men's and women's triathlon have been a part of the Olympics since the 2000 Games in Sydney, Australia, and most of the World Cup races staged for professionals are run over this same distance. Nowadays, every major city hosts a triathlon as well as a marathon, and most of the popular big city triathlons such as New York, Chicago, Washington, and Philadelphia feature an Olympic distance race. These events draw thousands of competitors.

World Triathlon Corporation (WTC), IRONMAN®'s parent corporation, has recently entered the Olympic distance game. They've linked several of the most prestigious Olympic distance events in the United States and abroad into a 5150 Triathlon Series.

This isn't surprising, the WTC tentacles are everywhere in the triathlon world. A few years back they introduced the popular IRONMAN® 70.3® Triathlon. These races involve a 1.2 mile swim, 56 mile bike and 13.1 mile run—exactly one-half of the distance of a full distance triathlon. Races of this distance have been around almost as long as the original IRONMAN race, but the IRONMAN 70.3 Triathlon is the new giant in town. Athletes can get a taste of the full experience with just half the work needed for a full distance triathlon.

Finally, if you struggle through all these lesser distances and your mind and body remain intact, another challenge remains: the IRONMAN Triathlon, the ultimate goal of many triathletes. It is a 2.4 mile open water swim, followed by a 112 mile bike, and a full 26.2 mile marathon.

There are only around thirty of these races held each year around the world. With around 50,000 people competing worldwide each year and just thirty official triathlons, it can sometimes get crowded.

■ ■ ■

There are many different types of triathletes. Some are men and women on the go, living in the fast lane, while others, like me, struggle to beat the cutoff time.

The competitors in a triathlon are divided into two broad groups: professionals and amateurs. The pros compete for prize money and represent only a small fraction of the athletes participating in a triathlon. The vast majority of entrants are amateurs, and they compete in five-year age groups; for example, males 25–29, females 30–34, males 50–54, and so on. These amateurs are known as "age-groupers" and an "age-up" rule is used for determining the specific age group in which each triathlete competes. Your age on December 31 is the age used for determining your age group for the entire year. If a triathlete is 25 on December 10, for example, he competes the entire year in the 25–29 age group.

No matter what the race distance, triathlons work pretty much the same. At registration you pick up a race chip and a race number. The chip is worn on a Velcro band, usually around your left ankle, for the entire race. On the left side it's unlikely to rub the chain ring of your bicycle. When you cross strategically placed timing mats, your time is recorded electronically. There's always a mat when you exit the swim and when you enter and leave the transition area, as well as at the finish line. In most of the longer races, timing mats are also placed at bike and at run turnarounds to make sure that no one cuts the course. With all the kicking and thrashing involved in an open water swim, it's surprising that these chips are rarely lost. The race director's favorite lament is "no chip, no time." They seem to spend much of their time obsessing over the timing chips.

Each athlete is assigned a race number that is worn on the bike and on the run, either attached to clothing or to an elastic race belt worn around the waist. Sometimes a similar race number is also affixed to the bike and to the bike helmet. In most triathlons, the race number is marked on the arms or legs (or both) with a black felt marker. Often the age of the athlete will also be marked on the calf. This allows athletes to spot age group competitors along the race route. If you catch up with someone on the bike or on the run in your age group, you can attempt to look fresh and relaxed as you try to motor past your rival.

With electronic timing being the norm in today's triathlons, I'm not sure body marking is all that critical. These chips are accurate to a fraction of a second. Yet, there's an almost mythical, ritualistic aspect to the body marking process. For some, it's like an Indian brave putting on war paint before a battle. For a few hours, the ordinary man facing the common stresses of modern life—credit card debt, car repairs, angry spouse—is able to enter a different world. He, along with a bunch of attractive women, gets to strip himself half-naked and cover himself with paint. What could be better than that? These body marks are a badge of honor that tell the outside world that this man can swim, bike, and run. He is not simply a middle-aged accountant or a banker, he is an athlete.

Sometimes these body marks can last longer than you would expect. Take my friend Frank, for example. He's single and in his late thirties, a man doing his best to stave off middle-age, trying to halt the march of time. I ran into Frank one Sunday morning at a group bike ride. He had finished a triathlon the previous day and I could still see a few faint body marks on his arms and legs. Frank is no fool, he did well at the triathlon and he wants everyone to know it. Later that same day, I saw him at the track with his girlfriend, a very attractive graduate student in her mid-twenties. To my surprise, Frank was strutting about with bold, sharp body markings. He had re-marked himself before meeting up with his girlfriend. Frank is a real alpha male, a man on the prowl, trying to stay atop the herd.

After body marking, it's time to check your bike and other gear into the transition area. This area is carefully cordoned off with only participants allowed inside. Helmet, water bottles, biking shoes, running shoes, race number, towel—you need a lot more gear than you do for a running event, and it's very easy to forget something. With no biking shoes or running shoes the race is impossible. Forget your bike helmet and you won't even get out of the transition area. Everything must be arranged and put in a special place in order to facilitate a fast transition from one discipline to another.

Before a triathlon, there are lots of things to check, and you have to have all preparations done well before the starting gun. If you cut it close and have a problem, like a flat tire or a missing shoe, you're in trouble. So you start early and invariably you end up with a lot of time to kill before the starting gun. An idle mind gives rise to a lot of self-doubt and anxiety. This is one of the worst parts of doing a triathlon, waiting and worrying, questioning your judgment and sanity.

• • •

As starting time approaches, the anxious herd lingers near the swim start. It's a time for meaningless talk, surviving the interminable minutes until the body's motor begins running and all nervousness disappears. Invariably the race announcer is chirpy, talkative, and a little annoying. "Six minutes to start; it's a great day; thanks to our many sponsors; everyone must have a chip," and on and on and on. Race announcers are like television weathermen, they both speak with an inane breeziness that sometimes makes you want to press the mute button.

Swimmers wear a colored swim cap that serves primarily as a safety feature; out in the lake or in the ocean, swimmers' heads are easier to see when bobbing in and out of the waves. Sometimes different swim cap colors distinguish women from men, pros from amateurs, or different age groups.

If the water is cold enough, athletes are allowed to wear wetsuits. These neoprene rubber suits fit very snugly and keep the swimmer not only warm but, more important, buoyant. Special models are produced for the triathlete with thick layers over the chest and abdomen for better flotation and flexible layers at the arm pits for easier arm movements.

My first experience with a wetsuit occurred a few years ago. I was headed to New York to visit my daughter and compete in the New York City Triathlon. It's an Olympic distance event and was my very first "big time" triathlon. "Wetsuits allowed," proclaimed the race website. I knew that I needed to borrow one to take along for my race, so I visited my good friend, Mike. He is approximately my height and weight, but there the similarities end. He's young, I'm old. He's got a lot of lean muscle, I've got a lot of flab. He's a great swimmer, I'm a horrible swimmer. He's done the IRONMAN® World Championship; this is the longest triathlon I've ever tried.

On race morning I am on the bank of the Hudson River, scheduled to start with the first wave of swimmers. I get another competitor to help zip me into the wetsuit. It feels like it must have shrunk on the flight up; I can barely breathe. A couple of cups of coffee that morning, a lot of pre-race anxiety, and a long wait at the start create a big problem. I need relief but there's nowhere to go.

A man does what he has to do.

The race goes well, I finish early, and my daughter thinks I'm a great athlete. She doesn't realize I started in the first wave of swimmers, well ahead of most competitors.

A few weeks later our local biking group had finished riding and we were telling tales, discussing race strategies. The subject of how best to stay hydrated came up. Everyone had their favorite tip, but we were all in general agreement: drink plenty of sports drink the day before and the morning of the triathlon. Be careful, don't get caught at the start of the race with a full bladder, you'll be uncomfortable and you'll lose time.

"That's no problem with me," I proclaimed. "I take a leak in my wetsuit right before the gun goes off." Everyone chuckled. Mike looked at me with a jaundiced eye.

Maybe I need my own wetsuit. I know I need a new friend.

■ ■ ■

Many triathlons start swimmers in different groups or "waves." For instance, men under 40 might start in one wave, followed five minutes or so later by men over 40, then women under 40 in another five minutes. This staggered start helps keep congestion to a minimum. Since everyone wears a timing chip, the computer sorts out the final times.

At an IRONMAN® event it's different; there's usually a mass start with all 1,500 to 2,500 swimmers going at the sound of a gun. It's much like swimming in a giant washing machine, especially at the start. Large, unpredictable waves crash about, other swimmers knock into you. Arms, legs, and elbows poke you from every conceivable angle. You feel shaken and stirred. Your brain tells you everything is fine, you're not drowning, but your body doesn't believe it. On occasion, swim goggles can be knocked off. My friend Ed is very nearsighted; he is so concerned about losing his goggles and his contact lenses that he keeps an extra pair of goggles around his neck, ready to snap into place should the need arise.

Swimmers follow a series of marked buoys and exit the water at the end of the course. There are usually water safety personnel in kayaks and other boats patrolling the waters to keep you from straying too far off course. Some IRONMAN® races actually have two or more laps on the swim; it's much easier to mark and monitor a 1.2 mile lap course than a 2.4 mile straight route. GPS technology makes today's swim courses more accurate than previously. Still, they are less than exact and must be re-marked each year, plus the waves and currents can change. As a result, your swim time in the same race can vary greatly from year to year.

Swimming in a straight line isn't easy, especially if the waves are high. Sighting is critical, and you may only get an occasional glance at the buoys from the top of a wave. Plus, your neighbor's straight line may not be the same as yours and he or she may come plowing across your bow. Sometimes it's uncontrolled mayhem, frantic pushing and shoving.

Once you exit the swim, gasping and staggering up the inevitable steep incline out of the water, you're into the first transition, or T1 as it is commonly known. The clock is running so you try to get to your bike and get out of transition as quickly as possible.

In most triathlons, once you're out of the swim you put on your helmet and biking shoes and head out of the transition area. It's a little different with the IRONMAN Triathlon. In these events, your bike gear is in a bag, and you have to retrieve the bag and take it into a changing tent. There is one for men and one for women. These tents are filled with panting athletes trying to change as quickly as possible. There are chairs provided to sit on while changing, but these chairs usually already have someone occupying them. Towels, wetsuits, bags, and other gear are strewn about.

In most cases there's very little changing in the changing tent. Athletes usually wear a one-piece triathlon suit or biking shorts under their wetsuit. Not many triathlons other than the IRONMAN series bother with these bags and changing tents. The bags do help you keep up with your gear and they do help keep down clutter. Since triathlon is a sport where people run around in the barest of clothing, the concern with public nudity is a little strange. I think the tents and the bags are part of the IRONMAN® experience, an attempt to create order out of race day chaos.

After the change, it's out of T1 and onto the roads. Time-wise the bike is almost always the longest leg of the race. Sometimes the roads are closed to vehicular traffic, sometimes not. Law enforcement officials are usually stationed at intersections for traffic control. Since many motorists absolutely detest spending their Saturday or Sunday morning stopped, waiting for cyclists to pass, this is an easy place for accidents to happen.

If the bike leg is long there will usually be aid stations with drinks and food. Cyclists toss their empty water bottles and pick up fresh ones or grab a banana or an energy gel. The trick is to grab the drink without stopping. It seems simple enough, but I've seen major bike crashes at aid stations, so I make it a point to always slow down.

Drafting on the bike is prohibited in practically all triathlons, including at IRONMAN races. The rare exceptions are the Olympic triathlon and the World Cup races. These draft legal events are for professionals only. Amateurs are required to stay roughly three bike lengths behind the bike in front. If you decide to pass the rider ahead of you, you must do so in 15 seconds, otherwise you may be penalized.

Once the bike is over it's back into the transition area for a second time (T2). A quick change into running shoes and it's on to the run course.

Switching from swimming to biking is effortless. The legs adapt quickly, and if you're tired, you simply quit pedaling and coast a bit. Since you settle in easily, you rarely need to practice this first transition. On the other hand, going from biking to running is torture. It's hard to even stand upright after leaning over the bike for such a long time. Coming out of T2 my back always feels like that of a man well into his sixties, I move like Frankenstein, and I feel like a fool for even trying to run.

When you begin running, your legs feel like Jell-O. The quadriceps feel as if someone has beaten them with a hammer. Every time I make the switch from biking to running, I think, "This is it, I can't run." It is a mental challenge to keep going. After a half mile or so things often get a little better, but it's never fun.

Since triathlons almost always start early in the morning, it's usually hot by the time the run comes up. Life is reduced to the basics—struggling from one aid station to the next, looking for a bit of shade, dreading the hills, counting down the miles, surviving to the finish line. With old age, running performance is the first thing to drop dramatically, well ahead of swimming or biking. There's no floating on the run, there's no coasting on the run, it's a constant, unrelenting effort.

In many ways, a triathlon is like a play with a badly written third act, a disaster to endure. The final curtain is the finish line; it's always good to be done.

Chapter 5

THE IRONMAN®
MYSTIQUE

NOTHING BEATS the IRONMAN experience. World Triathlon Corporation has created a great brand, one that they've nursed, protected, and promoted; a veritable golden goose that thrives in good times and in bad times.

It's not just a sporting event. It's a lifestyle, a mystical spiritual journey of self-discovery, a triumph over pain and adversity, a place where ordinary people achieve extraordinary things. Or so they say. No one is given to understatement in the world of the IRONMAN Triathlon.

The key piece of the puzzle is the actual name, "IRONMAN Triathlon." It's a magical word that conjures up images of heroic athletes covering vast distances, overcoming daunting physical and mental challenges, and struggling valiantly to reach the finish line. Nothing else comes close in endurance sports.

Much of the allure revolves around a question of supply and demand. There are only around thirty IRONMAN® Triathlons in the world. These races are held on six continents and serve the nearly seven billion people on our planet. The number of official triathlons varies as new venues are added each year and occasionally one drops off the schedule. By contrast, USA Triathlon, the governing body for the sport in our country, sanctions thousands of triathlons each year in the United States alone. If you want to do a triathlon you can probably find one very close to where you live, every state in the union hosts multiple races. IRONMAN races are another story, the choices are few, the opportunities are limited. It's not something you can decide to do on the spur of the moment.

While there are more than thirty IRONMAN Triathlons, there is only one IRONMAN World Championship, and it is held each fall in Hawaii. This is the most famous triathlon in the world, but not just anyone can show up and race; most athletes who compete in Hawaii qualify by winning an entry at one of the other IRONMAN events. These slots are awarded to the top finishers at the various IRONMAN races the preceding year. A few of the shorter IRONMAN 70.3® Triathlons also award slots to Hawaii.

The professionals earn slots as do the age groupers. Competitors in every age group, both men and women, have a chance to win a spot in Hawaii. The more popular age groups with many athletes have more slots available than those age groups with few competitors. There are a lot of men age 35 to 39, for example, but few women age 60 to 64. Regardless of the age, the competition for these spots is always intense.

Intense may be too mild a word. For some athletes, their very existence revolves around qualifying for Hawaii. Every workout is carefully dissected and evaluated. Eating habits, body weight, and heart rate are logged and charted. Things like family, job, friends, and faith go to the back of the line. It all goes into a big IRONMAN cauldron that contains the meaning of life.

The day following a qualifying race, a meeting is held and the slots are awarded to the winners. In some cases these slots "roll down" to the next in line if the winners don't show up at the meeting or if they choose not to go to Hawaii or if they have already qualified at another race. The qualifying athlete must be physically present, money in hand, to claim his or her slot, otherwise it rolls down to the next person.

WTC has another way to generate funds and, at the same time, give the average Joe a chance to reach the Promised Land. It's the annual IRONMAN lottery. Most competitors in an IRONMAN Triathlon have no realistic shot at ever qualifying for Hawaii. For a nice fee, they can join many thousands of other athletes hoping to win one of the approximately 200 slots awarded in the lottery. Not only that, if they pay a little extra, their chances increase.

It's a lot better odds than the Powerball, but it's still a long shot. Plus, there's one other crucial difference. In the Powerball lottery you win big piles of someone else's money, in the IRONMAN lottery you win the opportunity to spend big piles of your own money.

■ ■ ■

It's not all take, WTC gives back in a big way. In one area, IRONMAN racing stands head and shoulders above the rest of the athletic community. It has established a division to allow athletes with special physical challenges the opportunity to compete. Blind athletes, deaf athletes, amputees, paraplegics, and others with a variety of physical challenges participate in IRONMAN races around the world. This isn't a separate competition like the Paralympics; these athletes are integrated into the main event.

There are currently two different divisions for the physically challenged. In the handcycle division, athletes use a hand-cranked cycle for the bike and a special racing wheelchair for the run. This division has become so popular that athletes must qualify for the IRONMAN World

Championship at other events. The second category is for competitors with other special physical challenges, such as vision impairment.

If I had to name the one thing I most admire about IRONMAN® races and WTC, it is the special effort to incorporate the physically challenged into the triathlon community. These athletes are featured prominently in all aspects of the event. You see them before, during, and after the race, and they are part of the television specials. These outstanding men and women have overcome tremendous obstacles and are a true inspiration to everyone.

■ ■ ■

WTC is a great success story. It stages around thirty IRONMAN Triathlons a year, and each of these events can handle no more than 2,500 entrants. Unlike big city marathons, you can't pack thousands and thousands of athletes at the starting line, the logistics are too difficult. With thousands of people aspiring to earn the name of an IRONMAN finisher, the races commonly sell out the same day that registration opens. The demand is great. How can WTC open the event to more athletes? How can they bring more people into the IRONMAN tent?

WTC offered an answer with the IRONMAN 70.3® Triathlon series, a natural step for the athlete who is beginning to take triathlons seriously and dreams of becoming an IRONMAN athlete. Early on, finishing a full IRONMAN race may seem to be an impossible task, but attempting an IRONMAN 70.3 event is easy to imagine.

Currently, there are over fifty races in the IRONMAN 70.3 Triathlon series with new ones being added frequently. The events are staged around the world on six continents with a championship format similar to the IRONMAN series. The IRONMAN World Championship 70.3 is currently held in the Las Vegas area. Athletes qualify for this event by winning slots at other IRONMAN 70.3 races.

Communities around the world jump at the opportunity to host one of these events, paying directly and in kind for the privilege. An IRON-MAN 70.3® Triathlon is less cumbersome to stage than an IRONMAN race, the logistics are much simpler for race promoters. By late afternoon, everyone is finished, the course is clear, the roads are reopened, volunteer workers are done, and police are no longer needed. Both the full distance and half distance races are blue chip events for local businesses and governments. Athletes and their families come from all over the world to participate, bringing a level of prestige and a boom in tourism. The IRONMAN name is magic at any distance.

■ ■ ■

The appeal carries over into merchandise.

WTC sells a multitude of products at their races and online. All their events have expos with mountains of merchandise for sale. Naturally, this spot is called the IRONMAN Store and it racks up huge sales. The day after the race, the IRONMAN Store reopens with a different line of items. The shirts, jackets, jerseys, and such have Finisher boldly inscribed. This lets friends and families know that you not only entered but actually finished the event. I have seen long lines of exhausted athletes waiting patiently the day after a race, anxious to pick up finisher merchandise. After all, completing an IRONMAN Triathlon needs to be memorialized in every way possible.

Every major sporting event sells lots of merchandise, but there's one area where IRONMAN Triathlons have them all beat: the official tattoo. This is the ultimate triumph of marketing, an advertiser's dream, a no-cost permanent billboard for your product. It's there for the world to see and admire twenty-four hours a day, seven days a week, three hundred and sixty-five days a year. In their wildest dreams, the big ad agencies could never imagine such a bold stroke of good fortune.

A substantial number of people who finish an IRONMAN Triathlon have the official M-DOT logo tattooed on their body. In the triathlon world, the M-DOT is an ubiquitous icon that never fails to impress the impressionable. The tattoo is an indelible remembrance of your journey that you'll carry to your grave.

The tattoo is a great, symbolic event, but for an old guy like me, it's the most mystifying of modern styles. Throughout history young men underwent the rite to mark the passage from boyhood to adulthood. In today's society the IRONMAN® tattoo marks the transition from the everyday leisure life into the world of the athlete. People with one of these tattoos are not casual aficionados, they love this event. For many, their whole identity is wrapped up in the race. It's as if they're better people because of it, as though fitness equals character. According to these folks, the world is divided into those who have finished an IRONMAN Triathlon and those who can only dream. Since it's one of the most important events in their life, they want to commemorate it in a permanent way.

The experience is definitely unique and life changing, but that doesn't mean there is no room for improvement. I have some concrete suggestions to offer, things that will make this event even more mysterious and elite. To start with, I think we need a secret handshake, just like we had in my college fraternity. Once you complete an IRONMAN race for the first time, officials could pull you aside in a special secret tent and show you the handshake. This handshake would, of course, only be known and used by finishers.

Similarly, a secret password would be valuable for identifying fellow finishers in public. If you are in a bar and appear to be a finisher (thin, muscular, tattooed), someone could approach you and ask the secret password question. For example, "Do you know what time it is?" or, perhaps, "Where is the restroom located?" Any of these secret password questions would trigger the secret password reply: "Hell, yes, I'm an IRONMAN!" Both parties would then embrace warmly and exchange stories of their race experiences.

"The waves in that swim were tough."

"I never thought the bike would end."

. . .

An IRONMAN Triathlon lends itself to great drama. No one can fully grasp the experience. The media is filled with stories of people who overcame tremendous obstacles to become a finisher. Athletes survive horrible accidents, terrible diseases, drug addiction, and many other barriers on their way to the finish line. No sport celebrates the triumphs of regular people like this one does.

Old people like me can sometimes manage to finish. Then there are "Biggest Loser" kinds of stories where athletes go from gross obesity to IRONMAN veteran. The blogosphere is full of folks like the Marshmallow Man, the Couch Potato, and the Lard Boy who are training for an IRONMAN race. A couple of middle-aged friends of mine shed 50 pounds, threw away their blood pressure meds, and finished a race—all in 18 months. Now if I can just get them to quit talking about it all of the time. No obstacle is too great; a heart transplant recipient recently competed in an IRONMAN Triathlon.

Every IRONMAN story is interesting. I love and admire everyone who competes in one of these events, the details are always fascinating. There are few dilettantes in the world of this incredible race. There's no sense of entitlement, no room for whining or victimhood, no place for laziness. It's just a hard, time-consuming goal to reach, and that's what makes it so worthwhile.

The IRONMAN mystique lives on.

Chapter 6

IN THE POOL AND ON THE ROAD

I'M ALL in. After talking about it, thinking about it, ruminating about it, and pontificating about it, I've finally signed up for an IRONMAN® Triathlon. I've sent in the entry fee, bought my airline ticket, and booked my hotel reservation. There is no turning back.

I've entered the 2004 IRONMAN Brazil in May, less than four months away. Time is short but I'm determined. I can already see myself trotting across the finish line, modestly accepting the victor's laurel, describing the race in excruciating detail to family and friends, basking in the glory.

Choosing Brazil was easy. Entering an IRONMAN Triathlon here in the United States is too much of a long-term project for me. All of the American-based races are very popular and fill up a year in advance. I'm not ready to look that far into the future. I seldom know what I'll be doing next week, much less twelve months from now. I could be injured, unmotivated, swamped at work, in bankruptcy, dealing with family problems, living at an extended care facility.

With just a few months to race day I've got a rough idea of what kind of shape I'll be in. More important, I'll be in full-time training mode for weeks, not months. Some people are able to stay on a strict schedule for a full year leading up to the big event, but that's not for me. My attention span is short and my good intentions tend to weaken over time.

Besides, Brazil is a great place. Why should I go to Idaho or Wisconsin for a grueling triathlon when instead I can visit the land of the samba and the Carnival?

■ ■ ■

Now that I've signed up it's time to start training, but where do I begin? I know I need to swim, bike, and run and I know I need to do a whole lot more of each discipline than I'm doing now.

First things first, I'll start with the swim. It's the first event in the triathlon and if I'm not able to swim 2.4 miles in less than two hours twenty minutes then the bike and the run won't matter. Missing the swim cutoff would be a cruel fate, the worst ending imaginable.

For the past three to four years I've been doing a little swimming every now and then, and I've managed to finish a few triathlons, mostly the sprint distance. These races usually feature a swim of a half mile or less, so it didn't take a lot of training to get ready. My basic preparation for these sprint triathlons consisted of swimming around a thousand yards twice a week for two to three weeks before the race. In the winter I would often go for months without swimming at all. Obviously for a 2.4 mile swim I'll need to do a lot more training than a half mile twice a week. The big question is how much more?

I look on the Internet and I skim the triathlon magazines. There's a lot of advice floating around. Quite a few experts have written books and articles devoted to training for an IRONMAN® race. I also ask the few people I know who have done an IRONMAN Triathlon for their recommendations. There's no simple answer, the advice bounces all over the place. Some of it is practical, some of it is inspirational, some of it is useless. Even those athletes who have never done one have strong opinions. There are experts hiding behind every bush, waiting to point out my shortcomings.

The problem is that there's too much information, too many anecdotes. Besides, how relevant is the advice? None of the athletes I speak with are in their sixties like me, none are even in their fifties. There just aren't that many triathletes of my age to draw upon. My experts have Mercedes bodies with Porsche hearts and lungs, but I'm an old Volkswagen chassis with a lawnmower engine. What works for these young guys may be a bit too much for me. These days a hard workout sometimes leaves me feeling like someone has walked over my grave.

I read all the various training programs that I can find. Lots of famous triathletes have devised detailed training programs that can be individualized for any athlete. These programs are not simple, though. They talk about various zones and heart rate levels and such. Some training programs are like a tutorial on the physiology of exercise. For me, it's like a return visit to medical school.

None of the training plans say something simple like "swim this number of yards this number of times a week." Instead, there are a lot about warm-ups, drills, strokes, intervals, intensity, and things like that. Some programs measure workouts in time, while others measure them in distance. It's hard for me to know how long these training sessions will take. A good swimmer needs only 30 minutes to finish a workout that takes me over an hour.

All my friends and acquaintances who swam on a swim team growing up are much faster than me, so I ask them for advice whenever I catch them in the pool. They take pity on me and give me lots of tips.

Rotate with your hips, don't cross over with your stroke, your legs are sinking, your head is too high. In swimming, form trumps function. I try to incorporate their advice but it doesn't seem to make me any faster. It's hard for me to think and swim at the same time. If I correct one error, another pops up to take its place.

In the end, I decide to convert the detailed advice on swimming into a rough number of yards per week. I add up all the yards in the various plans and then divide the total by the number of plans. The magic number turns out to be 6,023 yards per week. A pleasantly precise number that sounds like something I can do. I've been covering around 2,000 yards a week, so I decide to start swimming three times a week instead of two, and I gradually increase my distance each week.

It all seems to work out pretty well, the more I swim the easier it gets. I'm slow, I make a lot of waves, I've got poor form, but I'm better than I used to be. Once a week I'm at the pool at 5:30 a.m. for my long swim session. In a couple of months I've got that long workout up to two miles.

These long sessions are very monotonous; swimming is the ultimate form of sensory deprivation. The same scenery, back and forth, lap after lap, a mind numbing immersion in a blue-green world. I don't seem to get tired, I just get bored.

When I glance at the swimmers in adjacent lanes, I'm often amazed. A middle-aged man, 40 pounds overweight, whizzes past. He is shaped like a big marshmallow but he has no trouble repeatedly lapping me. Some days a tall, young, muscular guy who resembles Michael Phelps swims next to me. We do lap after lap at almost the exact same speed. I tell myself I'm giving Michael Phelps all he can handle. Unfortunately he's not Michael Phelps, he's just another slow swimmer. I find out later that he first learned to swim only three months ago.

Since the swim leg of an IRONMAN® race has a 2 hour 20 minute cut-off time, anyone not out of the water by then is disqualified and not allowed to continue. I can make the distance in the pool in about 1 hour, 45 minutes, so I should have a little cushion in the race. Still, I'm a little concerned. In the pool, everyone stays in the proper lane, during the race it's every man for himself. Pushing and shoving are the rule; open water swimming is chaotic and jagged.

Since I have a mild amount of nearsightedness, corrective lenses help me see a little better at a distance. I want to be able to pick out the buoys in the ocean, so I don't end up swimming across to Africa by mistake. A search on the Internet turns up an inexpensive pair of swim goggles with my prescription incorporated in the lenses. A little tint also helps since the swim is at daybreak and the rising sun could be a problem.

The main item I need to buy for the swim is a wetsuit. Since they are rarely needed in the warm waters of Mississippi, nobody sells them in my area. I check out several ads in the triathlon magazines and I search the Internet. The wetsuit manufacturers are marketing geniuses, they offer three basic models: Fast, Super Fast, and Ultra Fast. How can I lose?

I phone the 800 number, tell the man my height and weight, explain that I need a lot of help, and give him my credit card number. Three days later an Ultra Fast wetsuit arrives in the mail. The next morning I wear it for a swim in the pool. It's great news, my legs no longer sink. I'm horizontal in the water, I don't even need to kick. I'm going so much faster that I inadvertently bump into the wall at the end of the pool.

I've made the best investment a slow athlete can make, I've bought speed. It's money well spent.

■ ■ ■

Next, I've got to figure out my plans for the bike. I know I'll have to be more structured, more disciplined if I'm going to complete the race in Brazil. I survey all the training plans, and I perform a detailed statistical evaluation, using the same mathematical formula that I used for the swim. However, a major question arises. In figuring out my bike mileage, should I use the median number of miles or the mean number of miles? This is an unexpected obstacle, and I'm wracked with uncertainty. I ask my friends at the health club, I start to call the League of American Bicyclists; no one seems to know, some even laugh at me. Ultimately, I use the mean instead of the median and that magic number turns out to be 122 miles a week. Fair enough, that's one long bike ride a week plus one or two additional short rides.

The bike leg of an IRONMAN® Triathlon is 112 miles, so I need to work in a couple of 100 mile–plus training rides before race day. In the past, I've done several 50 to 75 mile bike rides, so this seems in reach.

Early in my bike training I have to make a key decision. Am I going to do these long bike rides by myself, or am I going to do them with the Big Guys? During the actual race, I'll be all alone on the bike. With my slow swim time I'm certain to be at the back of the pack at the start of the bike leg. There's no drafting allowed, no riding in packs. The wind will be blowing directly in my face and the task of climbing hills will be mine alone. I estimate that I'll need around 7 hours to finish the bike, but who knows. I've never ridden that far and there are so many variables on the bike; heat, wind, hills, all are potential problems. There's a lot to worry about.

While training alone can be daunting and difficult, training with the Big Guys is often fun. You're in a group, tucked out of the breeze, hugging the rear wheel of the rider in front of you, your mind and body are on autopilot. You're going fast with a lot less effort. The Big Guys do the work, you're the follower.

In some ways, the Big Guys are like a beautiful woman. They can be warm, exciting, entertaining, even seductive. "Hey, John, come go with us, we're not riding that far." "You're doing great, I'm glad you decided to come." "You're riding well, when's your next race?" On occasion you forget that they're doing the work and you're riding in their slipstream. You actually start to believe that you're improving with age. In reality you're barely hanging on, riding just a few bike lengths in front of the Grim Reaper.

On the other hand, riding with the Big Guys can also feel cold, distant, even cruel. "Are you sure you can ride that far?" "Where the hell have you been? We've been waiting 15 minutes for you to catch up." "Try to keep up. We've got to get back before lunch." Some days there's little mercy for the slow and weak, you're reminded that you're in over your head. You struggle to keep up, eventually drop off exhausted and depleted, and hope for a better day in the future.

Unfortunately, the Big Guys are often forced to treat me as a special needs case. In my mind my old friend Butch has accrued tremendous moral capital. Whenever I'm dropped by the biking group, he comes back to get me, places me one inch from his rear wheel, and eases me back to the pack. As far as I'm concerned, this is a noble humanitarian gesture, like feeding the starving children in Darfur. It's generous assistance from a kindhearted man to an old hearted man.

As fun as it can be training with a group, I have to face reality, there'll be no Big Guys to shepherd me along in Brazil. They'll be long gone by the time I finish the swim and head out on my bike. Being a permanent member of the rear end group isn't fun, but it is something I'll just have to deal with.

It's settled. I'm going to do my long training rides alone. I wear my solitude as a badge of honor, no Big Guys, no drafting, just me and my bike.

■ ■ ■

It's late February when I officially start my IRONMAN® training program. Less than three months to race day. The weather is still cold in Mississippi and I don't have much experience riding in winter. Running in cold weather is great, there is no overheating, no dehydration. By contrast, cold weather can pose a problem when biking. It's hard to stay warm, and hypothermia is a danger. Several of my friends tell me I should try to bike inside instead of fighting the cold weather. It's a much more humane way to get a good workout, they say.

That makes sense to me, so one day I try the stationary bike at the local health club. It feels terrible. I move the seat up, down, in and out but I can't get comfortable. Next I decide to buy a trainer, a couple of hundred bucks for a curious-looking device that attaches to my own bike. It allows me to sit on my bike inside my den and pedal like a demon without moving an inch. This turns out to be the most boring thing I've ever done in my life. Swimming laps seems positively thrilling compared to riding a trainer. Sometimes I watch television, sometimes I read, sometimes I go solo with my iPod, but nothing seems to help. Time moves at a glacial pace. Minutes seem like hours. If this is what immortality consists of, I don't want any part of it. Saint Peter said it best: a day is like a thousand years. I've had my fill of the trainer. I'm doing all of my biking outside.

I start out one Saturday morning at daybreak with the temperature in the low thirties. My tires are pumped and my water bottles are full. I've got on so many clothes that my wife tells me I look like the Michelin Man. The wind and light drizzle feel like razor blades on my exposed face. There are just a few cars about and absolutely no cyclists; it's a dog of a day.

Some thirty miles south of town I'm alone on rural roads. It's mostly pasture and crop land with a few rolling hills. This is the rural South, the fields and forests broken only by an occasional house or trailer. The wind picks up but I'm still hanging tough. After all, I remind myself, I'm a budding IRONMAN® triathlete, I have to be able to handle anything.

An old, red pickup approaches from behind and a man in his sixties rolls down his window and flags me down. "Have you seen my bull?" he yells out, the sound disappearing in the wind.

I'm a little startled but I slowly recognize the voice and then the face. It's one of my patients, a man I've seen for years in my practice.

"Cecil, what's going on?" I ask. He stares at me, looks through my layers of clothes, discounts the funny looking bike helmet, and offers a glimmer of recognition.

"Doc, what the hell are you doing on that damn bicycle? Can't you afford a car? Hey, I'm looking for my bull, he got out. Have you seen him?"

Cecil can't be joking. Who would be driving around on a day like this just for the fun of it? What kind of bull would leave the friendly confines of the pasture or barn to go meandering about in the rain and cold? It doesn't make a lot of sense.

"I haven't seen him, but I'll keep an eye out," I reply.

Cecil offers me a ride home, but I beg off. I tell him I'm training for an IRONMAN® race. He's not too sure what this, is but he doesn't seem too impressed.

I'm wet and cold so I continue on, glad to get my motor running again, hoping to warm up, rethinking my IRONMAN journey, wishing I wasn't so dedicated. Once you're out in the boondocks on a bike you're committed, you have to get back home one way or another. I know I could call my wife on my cell phone and ask her to come pick me up, but by the time she arrived I'd be frozen solid. So on I go, trying to pedal a little faster, wishing for a little sunshine.

A half mile later I turn right onto a small country lane. This is a short cut that should enable me to get home a little quicker. I go another half mile or so and suddenly there he is in the middle of the road, twenty-five yards away, Cecil's bull, El Toro himself. An impressive beast, he must weigh tons. This is a real Big Guy, and he isn't riding a bike, he's staring right at me.

This bull is gigantic and he's blocking the road. If I knew how to ride a bicycle backward, now would be the time to do it.

I slowly stop my bike, trying to do all my movements in a deliberate, non-threatening way. I smile at the bull, hoping to project courage and confidence rather than fear. This bull has probably seen very few men on a bicycle in his day. Maybe he's as taken aback as I am, but then again maybe he's not.

I swing my bike to the left attempting to turn around and head in the opposite direction. El Toro sees me moving and scampers backward for a few yards. For a moment I think he's ready to charge, but he's really moving away from me. I start up again and once more, he backs away.

It suddenly dawns on me. This bull is afraid of me. Maybe he's heard I'm a big-time triathlete. News travels fast in small, rural counties.

Our little stop and go game continues. Instead of turning, I advance a little and El Toro retreats. I've forgotten how cold I am, bravery does indeed warm the blood. I feel like a courageous matador facing off a dangerous bull. It's like an Ernest Hemingway novel set in Mississippi with me as the protagonist. Is that the sun starting to rise?

We've probably gone less than 200 yards when I spot a break in the fence lining the pasture on my right. It looks like the bull has stepped on a weak spot in the fence, crushed it with his huge body, and walked right out onto the road, oblivious to the oncoming bicycle traffic.

I move to my left on the bike, then swing back toward the right. The big brute lumbers toward the break in the fence. A few more passes and he is through the opening in the fence and back into the pasture.

There, I've done it, my first successful bull roundup. Hemingway would be proud. This bull is back where he belongs; South Mississippi can finally rest easy. I can already see the headlines: "IRONMAN® CONTENDER INTIMIDATES MONSTER BULL" or perhaps, "BRAIN TRIUMPHS OVER BRAWN."

I'm still congratulating myself when I run into Cecil a bit later. I'm grinning, puffing out my chest, almost strutting. I describe what I did, omitting no details, maybe even embellishing my story a bit.

"Damn, Doc," he says, "you must have grown up around cows."

I'm still brimming with pride a few days later when Cecil and I again cross paths. He lets me know in a nice way that I've done battle with his polled Hereford bull. Polled Herefords are a breed of hornless beef cattle known for their docile temperaments. They are especially mild-mannered and easy to handle, the kind of bull everyone loves.

What a letdown. My monster has turned out to be one of the friendliest cows in the country. This big brute is the Ferdinand the Bull of South Mississippi.

. . .

Over the next couple of months the weather begins to warm, the countryside becomes green, and the bulls stay at home where they belong. There's just one problem, it's my old bicycle. I'm riding an aluminum bike, and I wonder if I couldn't do a little better. Aluminum is definitely better than steel but none of the Big Guys ride aluminum bikes. Most of them have sleek machines with frames made of carbon fiber or titanium. These bikes sport fancy aerobars with gear shifters on the end, and they're as light as a feather, many have giant disc wheels on the rear. They're space age machines. My bicycle is an embarrassment, old and outdated, a tin can, a bucket of bolts, a leftover from the *Leave It to Beaver* era.

Racing on an aluminum bike is like entering the Kentucky Derby on a mule, I tell myself. It's like bringing a knife to a gun fight. This isn't entirely true—an aluminum bike is only slightly slower than a carbon bike—but these are some of the many exaggerations, misrepresentations, and lies that I use to justify buying a new bicycle.

New bike fever is very similar to new car fever. Each day you think of yet another reason to purchase a new bike. Any one of these reasons alone is more than enough justification to spend the money.

"I've been training hard, I deserve the best equipment." "My buddies playing golf are spending a lot more money than I am." "The kids are out of the house, it's time to get what I want." "This new bike will last so long that I can take it along when I go to the nursing home."

After several days of back and forth, I decide to visit the showroom and check out this year's models, an impressive row of thoroughbreds built for speed. I head to the local bike shop to see the owner, my old friend Drew.

I've known Drew for a long time. He and I would sometimes run together back in the 1970s, a time when the heart, lungs, and legs seemed to work as originally designed. Through the years Drew has evolved from a runner to a triathlete to a cyclist. He spends most of his days working at his bike shop, but he has managed to remain lean and fast.

Drew is a man of few words, not prone to praise or hyperbole, but I'm an eager customer and I want to be sold. So, I start tossing out open-ended statements hoping that he'll encourage me to buy a new bike.

"Drew, I sure wish I could improve my bike time. I'd do anything to pick up a little speed." "I've heard some of the newer bikes can make you go a lot faster." "Steve got a new bike recently and now he's way ahead of me."

I'm all but begging him to tell me I need a new bike. If he'll just dangle the hook, I'll bite. All I need is a little encouragement.

Drew, an honest man, knows I'm asking for something he can't deliver.

"John," he says, "you don't need to upgrade your bike, you need to upgrade your body. A new bike might help you a little, but not much." I'm disappointed but not deterred.

"That sounds great," I reply. "I'll take it. I'd like the black one."

A few days later I've got my top-of- the-line carbon fiber bike. It's worth a lot more than the old pickup truck I carry it in, it may be worth more than my IRA.

My wife wonders if I haven't gone a bit overboard with my new purchase, if I haven't invested more than I should on my new wheels. She may be right but I quickly set her straight. In a moment worthy of Jerry Springer, I tell her, "If loving my bicycle is wrong, then I don't want to be right."

She's not very amused.

A new bike helmet and biking shoes follow and I have the second leg of the triathlon all taken care of. The tab for this little project is growing by leaps and bounds; my credit card is under as much duress as my worn out body.

. . .

My training program is finally taking shape. I've got a handle on the swim and the bike and that leaves only the run.

I feel a little more confident with the running preparations. Years ago I ran several marathons. In those days it would take me at least 50 miles a week to prepare for the 26 mile event, but that kind of mileage is impossible for IRONMAN® training. It's too many miles, too much time. Even the Big Guys recommend a lot less.

I decide to shoot for 3 to 4 runs a week with one being at least 10 miles long. I plan on increasing this long run each week, eventually reaching 18 miles. Most weeks I should be able to average 25 to 30 miles of running.

Fortunately, I don't need any special gear for running; thank goodness they don't make carbon fiber running shoes. I've tried lots of models of shoes over the years, and I now look for as much cushion in the heels as possible. Instead of wearing one pair of shoes until it wears out, I rotate two or three different pairs. This seems to keep my legs fresher.

Elastic shoelaces are another necessity. They allow shoes to slip on and off quickly with no tying or untying, which makes for a faster transition. Socks and shorts are simple and inexpensive. I'm in good shape, I've got all the gear I need and I've managed to avoid bankruptcy and divorce.

. . .

I've created the basic 101 training program for completing an IRON-MAN Triathlon and it's as narrow as it is deep. My regimen consists of swimming, biking, and running but not much else. It's a plan that's numbingly unimaginative and middle of the road; I'd have a hard time selling it to anyone. There's so much more I could do to prepare for this but I'm trying to keep my training as specific as possible. If I want to be a better swimmer, biker, and runner, I need to practice swimming, biking, and running. What could be simpler?

Unfortunately, I learn that it's not that easy. Swimming, biking, and running to near complete exhaustion is just the beginning, it's nowhere near enough to become a finisher. My friends tell me I need to consider weight training, yoga, Pilates, massage, meditation, stretching, and so on. This list seems endless, there's barely time for eating and sleeping. If I do everything recommended, I'll probably need to set aside some time for marital counseling. Still, I've never done an IRONMAN® Triathlon and I've got a nagging fear of the unknown, a dread of being unprepared. So I decide to check out some of these other essentials.

One day I visit the local health club and take a peek inside the weight room. It's an intimidating place full of big men with massive biceps and bull-like necks. Most of the time these boys toss around huge barbells and make loud primate sounds. Any one of these great discs of iron would crush my frail body in a second; just watching them makes me a little nervous.

Across the hall it's a gentler story. I glance in on a quiet, dimly lit room full of thin, attractive women. They're dressed in colorful outfits, stretched out on thin rubber mats, obviously at peace with the world. There's not a man to be found. These ladies are stunningly flexible, some seem to be scratching their ear with their big toe. Their movements are smooth and natural, seemingly effortless. This is yoga land, the world of tofu, organic foods, Jane Austen novels, and the Toyota Prius®, a place where the mind triumphs over the body. These women have their lives under control. It's no place for me; I can barely scratch my navel. I decide to stick with swimming, biking, and running and hope I can muddle through.

■ ■ ■

All of this training turns me into a morning person, early to bed and early to rise. I've always been more of a rooster than owl, but the pattern becomes more pronounced. I have no trouble falling asleep each evening, in fact, I have trouble staying awake. Each night before I turn in I have great plans for the following day. I promise myself that I'll do a long run or a hard bike, or a solid brick workout. Somewhere between dusk and dawn my determination disappears. Still I plug along usually doing less than I planned the night before, occasionally doing more.

The spring mornings are fresh and crisp and working out takes on a rhythm of its own. Some days are hard, some routine, and a few are easy. I go to work fresh, fortified with Starbucks coffee, eager to see patients, looking forward to Brazil.

I still have a job and family (at least for the time being) and there are only so many hours in a day, so I continuously try to simplify my training. I'm looking for that magical balance between too much training and too little. Life seems to get more complicated with time and it doesn't get any slower.

I decide to skip personal coaching even though I know that I would be a much smarter and a much better triathlete if I went this route. I don't have the time or the motivation and I'm too old to have a coach. The last time I had a coach was in my high school days. Back then, if I didn't try hard I had to stay after practice and run wind sprints. If the coach got really mad at me he'd take out his paddle and give me a half-dozen licks on my bottom. Times change. No one doles out corporal punishment anymore, especially to a man in his sixties, but I'm still not ready for a coach.

Over the years, several of my friends have hired personal coaches. They are constantly writing down workouts and goals, spending time on the computer, and chatting on the cell phone with their coach. If they miss a workout their life seems to become unraveled. They worry about every morsel of food they put in their mouth. Two workouts a day are the norm, there's little time for pleasure.

Sometimes this sport seems like a crack house for people addicted to exercise. It's certainly the dominant focus of their life; their coach becomes their psychiatrist and priest, their spiritual guide, a surrogate messiah. Coaches amplify, I want to simplify.

A personal coach provides you with a detailed road map to IRONMAN® success, you've got someone to answer every question and solve every problem. I'm like most men; I don't have a map and I hate to ask for directions. I hope I'm headed the right way.

Everyone tells me an IRONMAN race is a mental as well as a physical challenge. I'll have to admit that most of the time I'm not sure if I'm coming or going, my life is far from serene. Still, I am not doing anything special to get myself mentally ready for this triathlon. I try to focus on the positive and I try to avoid negative thoughts in general. I'm pretty good at identifying what I can control and what I can't and I try not to worry about something I can't do anything about.

If something good happens to me, I try to internalize it and build on it. I try not to take guilt trips. Once something is done, that's it. This all sounds like elementary psychology, the kind of stuff that Dr. Phil dishes out on a daily basis, but I've got one unusual quirk: As much as possible, I avoid setting goals. I have a goal of finishing this race and that's enough. I want nothing more and will settle for nothing less. No pie-in-the-sky projections for me.

All my life, for more than a half century, people have been urging me to set goals. When I was in elementary school my teachers would try to get me to write down my goals. Before school let out for summer my mother would ask me what my goals were for the vacation break.

"It's a good time to accomplish things you don't have time for during the school year," she would say. That was very true, but somehow these things to accomplish never included sleeping late, watching television, or going fishing.

I'm avoiding a laundry list of goals before setting upon my first IRONMAN competition. There are no special mental tricks for me. I can't meditate my way through this. I can't talk myself into finishing. It's all physical; I need to get to work. It's time to swim, bike, and run.

I know that there's a lot that goes into preparing for an IRONMAN® Triathlon and I realize that I'm not exactly an expert on full distance training. Nonetheless I've decided to summarize my program for anyone who is interested in learning what it takes to complete one of these insane triathlons. My program is very simple. If your training falls somewhere between the lower limit and the upper limit for each discipline, you can join the IRONMAN elite.

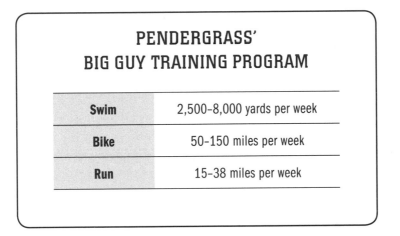

PENDERGRASS' BIG GUY TRAINING PROGRAM

Swim	2,500–8,000 yards per week
Bike	50–150 miles per week
Run	15–38 miles per week

ATLANTIC
OCEAN

SÃO PAULO •

• RIO DE JANIERO

★ FLORIANOPOLIS

BRAZIL

Chapter 7

ADVENTURES IN SOUTH AMERICA

BRAZIL

THE RACE day is just around the corner, and I can feel the anticipation and the anxiety growing. In no time at all the big day will be here and I'll have my chance to become an IRONMAN® finisher.

With three weeks to go, I've entered a triathlon in Panama City, Florida. It's exactly one-half of what I'll do in Brazil so it should be a good solid workout, a soft launch into the world of IRONMAN racing, my last hard day before the big event. After this race I'll cut back dramatically on my training. No more six hour bike rides, no more 5:30 a.m. swim sessions, no more muscle-killing long runs. I'll take more days off in the next few weeks than I've done in many months.

My friend Steve and I head down to the Florida Gulf Coast a couple of days before the race. We're booked at the host hotel so we've got a three night minimum stay. This hotel has been the headquarters of the race for many years and they're especially adept at extracting maximum dollars from poor, nervous triathletes like Steve and me. We're so scared that we do everything we're told without complaint. Steve and I have fear baked into our nature.

When we check in, we find out that the hotel has added a few extra bucks to the nightly rate. In return for the extra charge, we have unlimited use of the telephone for local and long-distance calls. That's right, anywhere in the good old USA, anytime we want, for as long as we want.

One of the things I like about Steve is that he is a primitive, low-tech guy like me, neither one of us has ever been accused of being an urbane sophisticate. In fact, we were both born in the wrong century. I can remember back when you picked up a phone and the operator asked, "Number, please." I do have a cell phone, but I rarely use it. I never text and I damn sure don't take pictures with my phone. In my mind, that's what cameras are for. Steve says he has a cell phone, but I've known him for over 30 years and I've never seen any credible evidence of its existence. He has always had a wary disdain for technology. Steve once told me that he thought email was just a passing fad.

There's a lot of time to burn before race morning; registration and a trip around the race expo don't take very long. A short swim in the Gulf of Mexico to check out our wetsuits and we're done. We decide to stay inside out of the sun, keeping cool, resting for the big day.

Inside our room, Steve immediately hits the phone like a man possessed. It's like he has won the lottery or discovered a cure for cancer. He's calling anyone and everyone with his magical free telephone.

The conversations all go basically the same. First, Steve inquires about some relatives or friends and then both parties exchange some news. This goes on for a few minutes and then Steve proudly explains that he has free unlimited long distance calls as part of the extraordinary deal the hotel has given us. He then tells his listener that he is in Panama City to do a triathlon.

Next comes the explanation of what makes up a triathlon—swim, bike, and run—and then Steve describes how long the distances are. For most people the numbers are meaningless. A few seem to recall those days long ago when they used to run or ride a bike, but most have no idea of what's involved.

Finally, he hears the inevitable question: "Are you going to win?"

Steve carefully explains that while he'll certainly be ahead of me, he'll probably be closer to the last finisher than to the winner.

This dose of reality is usually unacceptable to his listener. Steve is exhorted and encouraged to hang in there. "You never know," they say, "the other athletes may have a bad day, they may have injuries or illnesses or accidents. You might finish first. Never give up." This is great advice from someone sitting on a sofa at home drinking beer, but it's pointless for Steve and me.

Afterward, we both laugh and speculate on what it would take for Steve to win. Maybe a fulminant cholera epidemic that providentially spares elderly men from Mississippi, or perhaps a massive earthquake that swallows the entire hotel while we're out eating supper.

It's really impossible. We figure that guys like Steve and I are destined for the bottom half. We can only dream of finishing first. Our day will never come.

Finally, though, I figure it out, there is a way for Steve to win. If I could only convince the race officials to take the total time that each athlete spends talking on the "free telephone" and subtract it from the finishing time, Steve would win going away. This man may not be much of a triathlete, but he sure knows how to take advantage of a free telephone.

■ ■ ■

Race morning eventually arrives and we're both well rested, although Steve's voice is still a little tired.

First up is a 1.2 mile swim in the Gulf. There's a big crowd of swimmers and some large waves but things go pretty well. I try to stay relaxed and I do my best to sight the buoys at the top of the waves. These round buoys seem like little red dots that pop up and down out of the water line like targets in a video game.

I'm comfortable for the entire swim, and in no time at all I'm out of the water and jogging up the beach to the transition area.

About 10 miles into the bike leg I hear the dreaded "whoosh" sound. For a couple of seconds I'm hoping and praying it's coming from the bike I just passed, but no such luck. That noise belongs to me. I've got a flat tire.

Triathlons aren't like the bike races you see on television. No one hops out of a car following behind me and hands me a new wheel. I'm on my own. I've got to change my own flat tire.

Quickly, I'm off my bike and struggling around on the side of the road as cyclists speed past. Everything seems awkward, I wish I had a stool to sit on. I fumble getting my rear wheel off, manage to loosen the tire, and remove the old tube. I check for a piece of glass or rock, insert a new tube, and inflate the tire with a CO_2 cartridge. It has taken a long time but I'm just about ready to get going again. Most everyone who passes yells words of encouragement. I'm hanging in there, I tell myself. So what if it takes 20 minutes to change a flat, I'll make up the time.

I've barely gotten back on my bike when "whoosh," it goes flat again. This isn't supposed to happen. I check my wheel to make sure that I didn't pinch my tube. A new tube and another CO_2 cartridge follow, but no luck.

Time rolls along but my bike hasn't moved an inch. I'm sitting on roadside gravel, hunched over, stiff as a board. As the day gets warmer and warmer, my frustrations rise. I borrow another tube but the problem persists.

Eventually a pickup truck comes by with a large sign in the window, "Bike mechanic." I flag him down, here's the help I desperately need. The driver doesn't have another tire, he doesn't have another tube, either. He doesn't even have a pump. He's not exactly a bike mechanic, he's really more of a guy with a pickup truck whose job it is to take people with broken-down bikes back to the transition area.

Discouraged, I load my bike into the pickup and settle in for the ride back to the start. Major questions fill my mind. How can I expect to complete an IRONMAN® Triathlon if I can't even finish half the distance? What if I have a flat tire in Brazil? How do you say, "Please fix my flat" in Portuguese? If our country can put a man on the moon, why can't we make a bike tire that doesn't flat? Good questions, but no answers.

Back in the transition area I dump my wounded bike and head out on the run. If I can't complete the triathlon at least I'll get a good workout. The 13.1 miles are difficult. I feel so slow that I seem to be crawling, not running. Struggling with a flat tire has done nothing for my body or soul.

It's a long, slow ride from Panama City back home, a journey filled with remorse and regret, almost funereal. I describe the sordid details of the weekend to my wife—Steve's love affair with the telephone, my bumbling bike repairs, the humiliation of failing to finish. She smiles, "It's just a race, nobody died. You need to grow up."

Life marches on.

■ ■ ■

The next couple of weeks pass quickly. I'm checking and rechecking, packing a lot of stuff to eat, trying to figure out how to load my bike in its travel case, hoping that I don't forget anything. I want to bring everything I could ever possibly need.

After all, I'm going to Brazil, home of the mighty Amazon River and the great tropical rain forest. I've seen enough movies and I know what to

expect. It's a great big jungle full of menacing threats—schools of dangerous piranha that can strip the flesh off a human being in seconds, giant
serpents that can squeeze the last breath of air out of a weak body like
mine, stone-age natives ready to feast on my old carcass. This is no trip
for a sissy. There's a good chance I may not come back alive.

But wait, I'm not going to *that* part of Brazil. The race is being held
at Florianópolis, one of the greatest places in the world, a modern-day
paradise. *Veja* magazine, a popular Brazilian weekly, called it the best
place to live in Brazil. *Newsweek* named it one of the ten most dynamic
cities of the world. Nature reserves, great surfing, wonderful seafood,
beautiful vacation homes, Florianópolis has it all. Everyone wants to
go there.

There are over forty beaches on the island and apparently they are
all populated by the right kind of people, the in-the-know crowd. No
riff-raff is allowed on Florianópolis. How do I know this? The hallowed
New York Times named Florianópolis its "Party Destination of the Year."
This designation isn't just for Brazil or just for South America, this is for
the entire world. Who knows who I'll run into on this trip? I need to
be prepared to have a good time. Needless to say, the *Times* described
the island and its night life in glorious terms, pointing out that "affluent
Brazilians and in-the-know internationals have taken the party to Florianópolis." This is amazing, I bet you have to agree to drink and dance all
night, every night, before they'll even let you on the island.

"In-the-know international," that must be me. I've always felt I had a
jet-set gene tucked away somewhere in my genetic code, waiting for the
right moment to be fully expressed. It has lain there dormant, unused,
mainly due to lack of funds, for a good half century. These people are the
very essence of wealth, class, and power. This is my kind of place, this is
the moment I've been waiting for.

Florianópolis, here I come.

■ ■ ■

I've got my Portuguese dictionary packed. Over the years, I've pecked away at learning foreign languages. Trying to master another tongue is relaxing in its own way, it's like working a crossword or solving a Sudoku puzzle. It's mental massage for the weak minded.

I'm pretty decent at French and can get by in Italian, so the switch to Portuguese isn't real hard. The grammar is the same, the words are the same, it just sounds different. I keep telling myself that I've never met a reflexive verb I didn't like, that the subjunctive is one of my favorite moods.

Getting into my Portuguese mode is a standard routine for me. Grammar books and a dictionary, plus listening to audiocassettes to and from work. Today's Internet resources make it even easier.

No one in my area speaks Portuguese, so I spend time talking to myself.

"Como vai o senhor?" "Muito bem, obrigado."

When I see my patients, I ask them questions in Portuguese—only in my mind, of course.

The overnight flight from Miami to Rio de Janeiro takes around eight hours. I board a nearly full plane; most everyone had come aboard at New York, the originating city. My first challenge is to slide in next to an enormous man, who practically overflows into my seat. He has to top out at over 300 pounds. When he talks, his whole body shakes and wiggles. I feel compressed like a sardine; I know by the time I get to Brazil I'll probably be six inches narrower in the hips.

His name is Tomás and he's the first Brazilian I've encountered. My Portuguese rises to the occasion.

"Boa noite," I say, *"Como vai o senhor?"*

"O senhor fala português?" he exclaims.

"Muito pouco," I reply. Just a little.

"Não falo inglês," he states. He doesn't speak English. In reality he does speak English, just like I speak Portuguese. To paraphrase Bill Clinton, it depends on what the meaning of "speak" is.

We may not be able to get a job at the United Nations, but no matter, we're off on an extended conversation, chatting back and forth, communicating remarkably well. Tomás gently corrects my Portuguese and I help him with his English.

We're barely off the ground when a flight attendant comes by. There's a rapid fire exchange between Tomás and the young lady, and soon a couple of cold cans of Antarctica appear, one for me and one for Tomás. How does Tomás know I like beer? Antarctica is one of the great Pilsner beers of Brazil. Like any good drink, much of the enjoyment is due to where you drink it. I'm on my way to the party capital of the world, so the Antarctica has got to be special.

Dinner soon follows with a couple more beers for each of us. Tomás and the flight attendant seem to have a good thing going. From time to time she'll look at me and I'll say, *"a mesma coisa,"* but otherwise I just smile and act like I understand the conversation.

I'm a little tired, my day started over sixteen hours ago, but my Portuguese seems to improve by the minute. I'm telling Tomás all about my upcoming race. I toss out the words *"natação," "ciclismo,"* and *"corrida"* (swim, bike, and run) with seemingly great precision. I even use kilometers instead of miles when describing the race distances. Numbers are always difficult for me and I'm not sure if I shortchanged or overhyped the event.

Tomás is only mildly impressed, if he's impressed at all. It doesn't matter, he catches the flight attendant's attention and another round of Antarcticas follows.

Tomás shares some of his story with me. He is 45 years old and lives in Curitiba, a city in southern Brazil. He's back from visiting a cousin and a few friends who live in Queens but work in Manhattan in the West 46th Street area.

I return from my third or fourth trip to the restroom while Tomás sits relaxed working on another beer. He hasn't stirred from his seat the entire trip. This man has a bladder capacity appropriate for a man of his girth.

Time passes and Tomás and I start to exchange a few jokes. He is mostly telling and I am mostly listening. After each punch line, Tomás laughs and laughs. His living space expands and mine contracts. My insides, including my bladder, are being put to the test.

I don't mind too much though; my wife says I'm an agreeable person after a few drinks. Besides, my Portuguese is getting better and better. I'm able to understand much more, my accent is greatly improved. I certainly feel more confident, more verbose. I'm no longer speaking the *Portuguese for Dummies* variety, I'm letting loose with the real thing.

Then it dawns on me. I've made a major finding, something so profound that it could change the way we live. I've discovered the Second Thermodynamic Law of Beer Drinking. The First Law, very well known at least since the time of Chubby Checker, states in a precise and simple way: the more beer you drink, the better you can dance. Thousands of college students can vouch for the validity and importance of the First Law.

My Second Thermodynamic Law of Beer Drinking is both basic and practical. It states: the more beer you drink, the better your foreign language skills. I've proved the Second Law to be true on this flight and I'll confirm my findings many times on this trip. I tell Tomás about my important discovery, but I think he misses the significance of my findings. He laughs, he thinks I'm telling him a joke.

Tomás and I part ways at customs in Rio de Janeiro. He moves a little slowly but seems no worse for the wear. Me, I'm happy to have my feet on solid ground. My bedtime was hours ago. I wonder why my head hurts, why am I so thirsty, why are my eyeballs sore?

I can immediately tell I'm in a great nation, a place that has its priorities in order. The main airport of the country's most famous city isn't named for a military leader or a politician or a scientist. There are no statues of forgotten figures. Brazil knows what is important. This airport bears the name of Antônio Carlos Jobim.

In a country known for music, Jobim is undoubtedly its most famous musician. He joined with Vinicius de Moraes and João Gilberto to popularize the great Bossa Nova sound of the 1960s. A unique fusion of samba and cool jazz, the Bossa Nova dominated the decade. Decades later, his most famous song, "The Girl from Ipanema," still seems to meander through my brain at the strangest times.

I like this music. It reminds me of a nice lounge—soft seats, dim lights, good drinks, and relaxing sounds. A place where the music complements, but doesn't overwhelm, the conversation.

I guess it also reminds me of the 1960s. What great years. In those days I could get out of bed in the morning without every part of my body hurting. I could cross the 9:00 p.m. threshold without falling asleep. No one was calling me to buy a Medicare supplement. Medicare hadn't even been invented. Life was cheaper and easier.

I can't live in the past, though. The future and all the IRONMAN® glory awaits. I've got places to go and things to do. The 1960s are history and Antônio Carlos Jobim is no longer with us.

Unfortunately, neither is my bicycle.

. . .

I grab my suitcase from the luggage carousel and then wait and wait for my bike. I search all the odd places where baggage handlers sometimes dump a big bicycle case. No luck, no bike. How can something so big be misplaced?

This is the biggest race of my life and I don't have a bike. I'm like A-Rod without a bat or Tiger without a putter (or more realistically, like my Uncle Fred without a hearing aid). I can't function. I want my bike and I want it now.

The man at the baggage claims office takes my information and tries to reassure me, "Not to worry, João," he says, "The people in Miami, he screw up. The bicycle, she will come to you. You should now go away."

"She will come to me? You should now go away?" My last beer was a good three hours ago and my Portuguese has slipped quite a bit, there's not much I can say or do. It's just another bump in the road. What else can go wrong?

Bad weather and flight delays conspire to stretch the day even more and I finally arrive in Florianópolis late in the evening. My bike is missing in action and my body feels like it has been run over by a truck. I know things have got to get better.

My first encounter with Florianópolis is not what I expected. The wind is blowing at least 35 miles per hour and the hotel looks nearly deserted. The in-the-know party crowd must have turned in early. I lay in my bed, too tired to sleep, and listen to the roar of the wind. Fast moving shadows of the palm trees outside my room dance across the wall. In Mississippi, this is known as a tropical storm. I'm not sure what they call it in Brazil.

The next day I read that the port has been closed because of strong winds and high seas. However, it doesn't seem quite as bad as the previous evening so I decide to go for a swim. I tiptoe out into the Atlantic and plunge in. There's a lot of up and down bouncing around and brisk waves pummel me like a punching bag. It's hard to tell what direction I'm going, will I wash up somewhere on the African continent? Is there such a thing as a salt water piranha? I'm beaten and discouraged, and I quit after just ten minutes. No bike, bad seas, not an auspicious beginning.

■ ■ ■

There are still a couple of days until the race and the weather forecast says conditions will get better. It's hard to imagine them being much worse. You could tell me that the world is coming to an end and I would believe it.

I know if there's one thing that will help take my mind off the bad weather, it's a tour of the bike and run courses. This drive will give me a preview of how things will look on race day and will give me some new problems to worry about. No bike. No problem. Strong winds. Who cares? I've got this horrendously long race course to fret about.

I cram into the back of a van with several professional triathletes as the tour heads out on the bike route. The big hills on the course prove to be no problem for the van, but I'm not sure how I'll do on race day. I'm no van, I've got an old motor without much horsepower.

If the Big Guys are scared, they're sure not showing it. They are brimming with unshakeable confidence. They laugh and joke and banter. They talk about all the IRONMAN® Triathlons they've conquered in the past. Their stories go on and on and so does the race course. From time to time I toss out a comment or two, but the Big Guys ignore me. They seem to be annoyed at having to breathe the same air as me.

Driving the race route of a long event, such as a marathon, can be very intimidating—twenty-six miles is no easy stroll. But touring the course of an IRONMAN Triathlon is not only intimidating, it's downright terrifying. More than 138 miles total, it takes hours and hours in a vehicle to take it all in. My legs begin to get stiff, my seat hurts, and I need to use the restroom. I'm getting worn out riding this far in a van. What will happen on race day?

I see lots of athletes out biking and running in the days before the race. Many arrived over a week ago and have been hard at work. I've been in a full taper mode for a while, doing my best not to overtrain. These guys are sweating while I'm resting in the shade. Am I too lazy? Is my Big Guy training program going to fail me? Who knows? I can only guess as the challenges and anxieties keep growing.

■ ■ ■

Two days before the race I'm near the outdoor swimming pool, using the large mats as a place to stretch and loosen up. I'm trying to make a 60-year-old body work and feel like that of a 40-year-old model. I'm grunting and grimacing and snorting and making all kinds of strange noises, when I'm joined by a young couple.

The man begins to do a series of stretches and is ably assisted by his absolutely gorgeous girlfriend. Their movements are long, deliberate, and protracted, they seem almost choreographed. Both have sculpted bodies with maybe three ounces of body fat between the two of them. This couple could be on the cover of a fashion magazine. They represent one extreme of beauty and physical fitness, while I represent the other extreme.

They're both from Argentina, and in their early thirties. Daniela is a physical therapist and is helping her boyfriend, Martin, prepare for the race. This is Martin's first IRONMAN® Triathlon and he tells me he is certain he can finish in under ten hours.

We chat a little in Portuguese but soon end up switching to English. Martin seems very dependent on Daniela, she directs the routine and he says very little. I try to be polite and I toss him a question every now and then, but Daniela and I end up doing all the talking. She tells me that Florianópolis is a popular vacation spot for Argentinians, and that they have been here several times before.

A little later Daniela offers to help me stretch and, of course, I eagerly accept. My range of motion is about one-fourth of Martin's but I'm not discouraged. Daniela pulls my leg this way and pushes it another way. My back is in a crazy position it hasn't seen in decades, my legs are begging for relief. It all seems way too much for my body. I can almost hear my bones creaking. After a few minutes of this routine, I beg off.

Daniela is a beautiful woman with a wonderful smile, and she keeps asking me these strangely phrased questions. "Does the gentleman feel less tense, more relaxed?" "Is this the gentleman's first triathlon?" "Is the gentleman staying long in Brazil?" "What does the gentleman think of Florianópolis?"

What is going on here, I wonder, I've never had this type of conversation before. Maybe Daniela is a specialist in the third-person singular. Who knows, maybe in Argentina this style of speech is used to address the elderly, a special mark of deference to senior citizens. I'm not sure.

It's not a problem, though, this gentleman doesn't mind at all. This gentleman is happy to answer all questions from Daniela. After all, this isn't Mississippi, this gentleman knows things are a little different here in the party capital of the world.

■ ■ ■

The day before the race is normally devoted to three things: attending the race briefing, checking your bicycle and other gear into the transition area, and increasing your anxiety level from "extremely nervous" to "unable to quit shaking."

I'm ready to check in a bike, but I can't. My bike still hasn't arrived, it's somewhere between Florida and Florianópolis in lost luggage limbo.

Ever since my arrival I've been searching for my bike. Several times a day I check with the hotel, call the airline, and badger the local race officials. I even look into renting a bike or perhaps borrowing one. There has got to be an extra bicycle somewhere in the country. I need help and I need it fast.

The local response is always the same. "*Senhor,* you don't need another bike, your bike will be here by race day." "You don't need to worry," everyone says with an absolute, unequivocal certainty. The sun will rise in the morning, the Amazon flows to the sea, your bike will soon arrive. They all treat me like an idiot for making these inquiries.

My fellow athletes are sympathetic but much less certain. They have all heard stories of bicycles being sent to the wrong city, being severely damaged by the airline, or even vanishing from the face of the earth.

These horror stories are very unsettling. I'm just a few steps from the crazy house.

The morning of the day before the race I stroll through the hotel lobby after breakfast. I didn't eat a lot, not much appetite. The last few days I've been living a life of quiet desperation, waiting anxiously for my bike. I wonder, will it ever show up or will I go to my grave with no bicycle? Much of my current world turns on important questions like this. An IRONMAN® Triathlon has a way of reducing life to its basics.

Suddenly, there it is. My bike appears unannounced in the lobby, nestled in its case, pushed over to the side against a potted plant, looking no worse for the journey, anxious to be reunited with an appreciative owner.

I take my bicycle up to my hotel room, quickly assemble it, and take it for a 10 minute spin, then I load it up and carry it to the bike check-in.

The whole process happens so quickly. One moment I had no bicycle, a few moments later I have the best bicycle in the world. It's a friendship renewed. Absence makes the heart grow fonder. I feel much better. I've got a bike. I've got a chance to become an IRONMAN finisher.

■ ■ ■

In the days before the race while waiting for my bike to arrive, I try to solve the riddle of the IRONMAN bags. It's like a Chinese puzzle with false starts, dead-ends, and detours.

At registration, each person receives five large plastic bags for use during the triathlon. Each of these bags is numbered and labeled and holds specific items; what goes in one bag doesn't belong in another. Mix them up at your own peril.

To start with, there's a bag to hold the clothing you've worn to the race start. After the race is over, if you're still able to dress yourself, you'll put on this same clothing to wear home.

Another bag is designed to carry the biking gear you'll need after you've finished the swim. Still another to store the running gear you'll require after the bike.

There's a special needs bag that is accessible midway through the biking course. You can pack special foods, gels, extra drinks, spare bike tubes. I wonder if I should use this bag to store my AARP card for safe keeping. I wouldn't want to miss those special senior discounts. There's a similar special needs bag for the midpoint of the run. It's a great place for some good snacks or a cold beer.

It's not enough to spend your free time swimming, biking, and running in preparation for a triathlon. You have to be a mental gymnast, shuffling and sorting, bagging and unbagging, hoping you've placed everything where it belongs. I think I've got the right things in the right bags, but I'm not sure. Where does this bottle of Geritol™ go? What about my Flomax™ tablets?

■ ■ ■

Race morning finally arrives. The hurricane-like winds that I experienced on arrival are a distant memory. The weather is great, temperature in the mid-50s, low humidity, just a little breeze. It seems like I landed in Brazil years ago but it has only been three days.

It's a solemn group in the men's changing tent. Everyone has finished their pre-race preparation. Most have slipped into their wetsuit and are waiting for the start. Nobody is laughing or smiling, many look worse than me.

There is no doubt a very difficult day is in store. There will be pain and suffering in varying amounts for absolutely everyone. No one gets a pass in an IRONMAN® Triathlon.

I spend much of this time praying to the Lord to help me survive and finish. My faith is plain and unsophisticated, I'm not above bargaining. If He wants me to drop those long Sunday morning runs and start spending more time in church I'll do it. If the money for my new running shoes needs to go in the collection plate, so be it. I'm very open to divine intervention.

It's going to be a long day and I need all the help I can get. "Let us run with perseverance the race marked out for us."

The swim course is made up of two laps separated by a short run on the beach. Each lap is supposed to be rectangular in shape but it's really hard to tell. The buoys are small and not in a straight line, making them difficult to follow. I decide to stay in a crowd; I feel as long as there are a lot of swimmers around me, I should be okay.

More than 1,000 athletes are off at the sound of the gun. I wait near the back of the pack and soon find a comfortable spot. The swimming is easy, this is the first event and I've had lots of rest in the last few weeks, so I have no reason to be tired. Soon, the butterflies are gone; this is the best I've felt since I arrived in Brazil.

The location of the buoys still has me a little confused so I choose the longest route to make sure that I don't cut the course. I'm not taking any chances. I've been behind the curve since the day I arrived. I'm afraid of making a mistake.

The first lap is done in around 52 minutes. I had hoped to be a little faster but I'm glad I still feel fresh. I'm about to start the second lap when the two race leaders emerge. They have completed two laps in the time it took me to finish one. These Big Guys strip off their wetsuits in no time at all and vanish up the beach. I wobble on unsteady legs before heading back into the water.

My second lap, not surprisingly, is worse than the first. A strong cross current develops and keeps pushing me laterally. If I want to reach a buoy straight ahead at the 12 o'clock position, I have to swim in the 2 o'clock direction. It becomes a chore to keep swimming in a straight line. I find I'm trying harder but going slower.

I'm delighted to see solid ground when I finally finish at 1 hour, 56 minutes. This has been a pretty hard swim and quite a few people missed the 2 hour 20 minute cutoff time and had to drop out of the race.

Soon I'm out on the bike, aiming to stay out of trouble. I've still got flat tires floating in my brain. It's hard to believe that less than 24 hours ago I wasn't even sure that I would have a bike to ride. Now I'm riding smoothly, almost on cruise control.

This leg of the race takes forever, sometimes even longer if you have a flat tire. Each of the two laps has three nice hills going out, a tour of downtown Florianópolis, and then the same three hills coming back. It's late morning on a pleasant Saturday in May, and many people are out and about shopping. The roads are full of traffic and there is just one lane blocked off for cyclists. Everyone in Florianópolis is tending to their own business; no one seems to notice the triathletes.

The first 56 mile loop goes by quickly. I've got fresh legs, they're working fine at present, but in the back of my mind I know they could reach their expiration date at any moment.

I'm really worried about getting dehydrated. Everything I've read and heard says drink, drink, drink, so I really press the fluids, alternating water and Gatorade™. This results in three pit stops on the first lap alone with no toilets available on the route. I stop on the side of the road, act like I'm alone in the Amazon rainforest, and go about my business. The passing motorists all honk; maybe they are paying attention after all.

One or two miles before the end of the first lap, the two leaders pass me on the bike. They're finishing the final lap. It's a very impressive sight. They are escorted by eight fully uniformed motorcycle police. The Big Guys, separated by a couple of bike lengths, are flying. Lights are flashing, sirens are sounding, these boys are moving. It's like the tortoise and the hare, but I'm under no illusion, this tortoise has no chance. The hares will win today.

As I head out on the second lap, I seem to handle the trio of hills surprisingly well. I'm some eighty miles into the bike leg and I'm still feeling decent. I think to myself, maybe I'm in better shape than I thought, maybe sixty really isn't that old. Each month I read the AARP magazine and learn that seventy is young, just a brief interlude before those exciting eighties. Still, I keep getting solicitations for a strange variety of products—long-term care insurance, hearing aids, trousers with expandable elastic waist bands. I wonder, will I ever need those old-timers goods? The way I'm feeling now, I could ride this bike all the way to the great transition area in the sky.

As I turn around and head back in for the final 30 miles or so, the reason for my burst of energy and optimism becomes obvious. A nice tailwind had popped up on the outward bound leg of the second lap and pushed me along. Now I have to fight the big hills coming back directly into a headwind.

I'm beginning to get tired; it's a long struggle, the hills are much steeper, there's no one to draft on. My seat is sore. When a senior citizen like me really needs help, where the hell is the AARP?

I glance down at my odometer, ninety miles in the bank. Hang in there. I ride and ride and ride. I must be near the finish. I look again at the odometer, 91.5 miles. The miles go by so slowly. Will it ever end?

It's around 4:00 p.m. when I finally arrive back at the transition area, some nine hours or so after I started. On the bike, I pass lots of runners, some heading out, others close to finishing. The winner has been done for about 30 minutes.

I hand my bike to a race official and head into the tent to change into my running gear. My back hurts, my legs feel like rubber. I'm all hunched over. I wish Daniela was here to help me, but I know she is probably back at the hotel preparing for Martin's post-race massage.

I struggle onto the run course and continue to encounter runners headed toward the finish. This is very discouraging. Why can't I be fast like them, why can't I be a Big Guy? Fortunately, I do see some other cyclists returning; at least I'm ahead of a few people.

Eventually my back loosens and I'm able to stand up straight. I've lost the hunchback shuffle, I no longer look like Quasimodo's long lost brother. The sun is setting and the air is crisp and cool as the shadows fall. It's very beautiful in Brazil. I run a few miles to the first aid station and stop for food and drink. I start up again, go for a short distance, and then stop.

My gas tank is empty; I don't have the energy to go very far at a time. I'm reduced to running a hundred yards or so and then walking for about twenty yards. There are still twenty-four miles to go and I feel awful. Run and walk, run and walk, there's no relief. My agony will last hours and hours; the hardest part of the triathlon has just begun.

So I putt along, trying to take food and drink, but my appetite just isn't there. Bits of bananas and swallows of water and Gatorade are the best I can do. As the night lengthens, things get progressively worse.

At one aid station I grab a cup from the table. It turns out unexpectedly to be a warm, thick chowder and I reflexively spit it out. The aid station workers laugh and laugh, this is probably the most interesting thing that has happened to them all day. This crazy old American doesn't know how to swallow his food, what's he doing in an IRONMAN® Triathlon? Take him back to the nursing home.

The miles click by at a glacial pace. Every step hurts. The course is marked in kilometers, and I have trouble converting the distance to miles. It's a very simple mental calculation but my mind is foggy and works no better than my body. I'm in survival modes and I really don't know what finish time to expect, maybe 15 or 16 hours, I just want things to quit hurting.

Eventually I turn onto the main street, with just one kilometer to go. I make a determined effort to run the full distance. As I head into the finishing chute, there are a few dozen people milling around, a handful yell words of encouragement and a few clap.

That's it. I'm done. I'm an IRONMAN finisher—14 hours, 20 minutes, 15 seconds.

• • •

If you ever want a super-sized serving of euphoria along with an even larger helping of relief, the finish line of an IRONMAN® Triathlon is the place to go. The feeling of accomplishment is indescribable.

I proudly accept my finisher medal and shirt and go to a nearby stretcher to lie down. I'm totally exhausted, every cell in my body hurts. The supine position becomes my preferred posture for thirty minutes or more. It feels good but I can tell my body is becoming rigid, my muscles are as flexible as a piece of concrete, so I have to move.

A helping hand gets me off the stretcher and points me to the massage tent. IRONMAN Triathlons are wonderful training grounds for massage therapy schools. There's a nearly inexhaustible supply of badly bruised bodies in need of relief and rehabilitation. Students get to see human musculoskeletal damage taken to an extreme, a classic example of dumb people doing stupid things to their body.

My student therapist is very nice. She asks what hurts and I reply, "Everything." She smiles. I know she has already heard that answer many times today.

Eventually, I gather my gear and head back to the hotel. I call my wife to report that she is one of the few women in town married to an IRONMAN finisher. She is genuinely happy and hopes that I've gotten this out of my system. "Don't worry," I tell her. "I'll never hurt like this again for as long as I live."

For the next six or seven hours I lay in bed too exhausted to sleep or eat. It's a strange mixture of joy and suffering. The feeling of relief and accomplishment is wonderful. I've paid the price in training and on race day. I'm enjoying the pain, I've earned it.

Many people with much better credentials than I, with much stronger legs, with a much younger heart, will never accomplish what I've done. I've been in the arena and the credit belongs to me.

■ ■ ■

The sun comes up and my appetite returns with a vengeance. My hand is getting worn out from patting myself on the back, so I decide it's time to eat. The breakfast buffet opens at 7:00 a.m. and I'm first in line, eager to make up for lost time.

If you like to eat and drink, there is no better place in the world to be than Brazil. The coffee is wonderful, it's rich and deep brown in color. It's served piping hot from large vats, usually accompanied by warm milk. I'm a longtime coffee addict and this is caffeine heaven for me. My friends at Starbucks would do well to buy all their coffee from Brazil.

This country has an endless array of fruits and vegetables. The commonly known oranges, tangerines, bananas, mangoes and papayas, plus a lot of other strangely named fruits like jabuticabas and pitangas. Beef, pork, lamb, and chicken, in all sizes and cuts, along with plenty of seafood, rice, and beans. It's all here.

It's a great time to dine, the laws of nutrition have been suspended. After an IRONMAN® Triathlon you can eat anything you wish, as much as you want, and not gain weight. This holds true for a couple of weeks, and it's a well-earned blessing.

I'll further test my nutritional theory later today, but first I'm on my way to a very important destination, the race expo.

The expo is the home of IRONMAN Brazil race gear. Dozens of ordinary things that would draw little notice in the normal world have been transformed into valuable must-have items, simply by the addition of the IRONMAN name or logo. If it says "IRONMAN," I probably need it. Most everyone else feels the same way.

I was handed a very nice finisher's shirt when I crossed the finish line. It cost me hundreds of hours of hard work preparing for the event plus thousands of dollars in race and travel expenses. Not a wise investment from a financial point of view. Still, I think it is a great tee shirt, more valuable than a Super Bowl® ring in my mind. I'll always treasure it and I may even ask to be wearing it when I'm buried.

Yet, at the same time, I realize this simple finisher's shirt doesn't do justice to my great athletic achievement. I know I was bringing up the rear of this race, and I realize the Big Guys would laugh at my time but this doesn't prevent me from buying two more tee shirts, a nice polo shirt, a pair of biking shorts and matching bike jersey, and a great coffee cup.

The evening is devoted to a meat lover's paradise, the churrascaria. This Brazilian-style steak house is making inroads in the United States and it's easy to see why. We Americans like meat and calories and the churrascaria has plenty of both. In fact, if there's a finer place on this planet to eat for ten bucks, I've yet to find it.

After a warm-up with the salad bar, patrons are served by passadores who continuously circulate with giant skewers loaded with cuts of meat. The various selections are grilled over charcoal or wood, and they are all delicious. This is southern Brazil and the gaucho tradition is strong and alive.

I like it all, but one particular skewer of meat stands out. The small, tasty, roundish cuts are wonderful. Golden brown, less than an inch in diameter, these delicious morsels are the perfect size, they seem to jump into my mouth. The passadore can tell that I'm enjoying his selection and he soon returns with another big serving. He smiles and pats me on the back. I think he's telling me that I'm a true man of Brazil.

We're all sitting at a long table enjoying the delicious food and large bottles of Brahma (another great Brazilian beer). Everyone notices my fondness for the tasty little nuggets; I stand out in a crowd of serious eaters. The passadore returns and I listen a bit closer to what he's saying. This time, it's as clear as day. "Dig in, don't let your chicken hearts get cold."

Everyone smiles. With no effort at all I've acquired a new name, a title appropriate for me in so many ways. You can call me Chicken Heart. These tiny hearts used to belong to some poor fowl before I started scarfing them down. In the poultry world, I'm now public enemy number one.

Chicken Heart is not exactly the same as being known as Braveheart, but it's probably the closest I'll ever come.

. . .

Although I've only been in Brazil for about a week, it seems like forever. So much has happened. It has been a time of anxiety and anticipation, followed by a Herculean challenge of finishing an IRONMAN® Triathlon and capped off with feasting and celebration. It's not exactly "Eat, Pray, Love," but more like, "Worry, Sweat, Eat."

This past week I've had some good conversations with Paulo, one of the local guys hired by our travel group to help make sure that things go smoothly. Paulo is in his early thirties and does a little bit of everything. He's a driver, baggage handler, tourist guide, philosopher, restaurant critic, observer of the opposite sex, and general factotum.

Paulo was there when I finished the race and helped carry my bike and gear back to the hotel. He has taught me a lot about how things work in Brazil. "Take your time," he says, "things will work out, it's never good to be in a rush."

Not bad advice for someone tackling his first IRONMAN race at age sixty.

Paulo knows I'm going to be spending some time in Rio de Janeiro after the race and he encourages me to look up his cousin, Eduardo. Eduardo is a tour guide, Paulo tells me, who knows the city inside and out. With him I'll be in good hands and I'll get to see the real Rio de Janeiro.

That sounds good to me. I have Paulo call ahead to let Eduardo know I'm on the way. I wonder if Eduardo knows that I'm an in-the-know international?

I've been booked into one of the great old luxury hotels that front on Copacabana Beach. It's a place of rich wood, thickly upholstered furniture, and loads of crystal chandeliers. Guests in bathing suits wander in and out and mix with staff dressed in dinner jackets. It's a strange mixture of exaggerated opulence and an informal trip to the beach.

Eduardo shows up the next morning. He is in his late thirties and a law school graduate. After several years of working at a bank, the hassle and stress became too great, and Eduardo decided to quit his job. He now does a variety of part-time tasks, including serving as a tour guide. Eduardo is married with two young children and he spends a lot of time helping his wife, who works full time, to care for the children.

We get along great. There's no tour group or tour bus. Eduardo and I travel the city by subway, by bus, and on foot. I'm eager to see as much as possible and he is happy to comply. He's pleased I'm interested in Rio and he tolerates and encourages my fractured Portuguese.

The city has a population of around seven million people with a density greater than Manhattan. It's a vibrant place with lots of street-side vendors hawking all types of goods. We go to most of the standard tourist sites plus a few unexpected stops. There is no rhyme or reason to our travel and we make many detours along the way.

Corcovado, the great central granite mountain of Rio, is stunning. The peak is topped by *O Cristo Redentor* (Christ the Redeemer), the magnificent Art Deco statue. Jesus Christ stands perched atop the city over 125 feet tall with perpetually outstretched hands, a beautiful symbol of the power and grace of Christianity.

We watch the monkeys play in trees of the forest reserve before ascending the mountain on the rack railway. The view is impressive from the top.

Rio's other great mountain *Pão de Açúcar* (Sugarloaf) is accessible via cable car. It sits at the mouth of Guanabara Bay providing a notable welcome site for those arriving by sea.

Eduardo and I not only go to the top of the city, we also visit the beaches of Copacabana, Ipanema, and Leblon; we see the old cathedral and the new cathedral (I much prefer the old one); we wander through a flea market and a food market. Each day brings something new and different.

One day we head to Santa Teresa, a charming hill top area of Rio, full of narrow winding streets and lots of what my wife and daughter call "cute little shops." The community is a favorite spot for artists of all stripes and colors and you can wander about and spend hours visiting the numerous studios and galleries.

We're not here to shop, we both have wives who are experts at the task. It's lunch time and we're here to eat feijoada, the national dish of Brazil. Eduardo swears by feijoada and tells me that he has eaten it at least once a week for as long as he can remember. He is enthusiastic, so I'm enthusiastic. When it comes to food, lead me to the feeding trough and I'll do my duty.

This restaurant definitely doesn't cater to the tourist trade. It has all the earmarks of a beloved neighborhood joint. A small dark place well off the main street with just four tables, it seems more like a stall opening onto the alley than a restaurant.

Feijoada is basically a stew of black beans and meat parts, mostly pork. It is usually cooked in a clay pot over a slow flame and takes a long time to prepare. Most restaurants will offer it only at lunchtime and only one or two days a week. Feijoada is a solid dish, with many large chunks of meat afloat in a broth. Several other side items are usually served with the main dish—rice, greens, and a lightly roasted cassava flour called farofa.

It's a rich and tasty confection. The beans and broth complement each other, and most of the meat is quite tender, having simmered for hours. Some pieces, though, seem a little tough. I have to chew and chew to break them up, but that's okay, nothing's perfect. I work through a large helping, happy to have another good meal.

Eduardo is proud of Rio de Janeiro and enjoys showing me the sights. He is the teacher and I'm the student. There is much to see and to do, but he saves the best for Sunday afternoon. He tells me this is what Brazil is about; this is the country's heart and soul.

Eduardo and I take the subway from downtown Rio to visit the great mother church of Brazil. We are not going to the Cathedral of Rio de Janeiro, we're headed somewhere much more important. We are going to the great temple of Brazilian soccer, Maracanã stadium.

Soccer, or *futebol* as it is known in Brazil, is the one great dominant unifying feature of the country. Regardless of class, race, or geography, everyone loves soccer. It's a vital and central element in Brazilian culture, probably more important than the Catholic Church or Carnival.

The subway car to Maracanã is packed with fans. We're going to the stadium to watch Flamengo take on a rival team from São Paulo. There are four major soccer clubs in Rio and Flamengo is probably the most popular. It's the team of the masses and it enjoys great support among the poor and the blacks.

Maracanã stadium is a giant, two-level concrete oval. Eduardo has gotten us seats in the less expensive upper level with all the blue collar hard core fans. The pitch is surrounded by a deep moat and seems very far away from our seats, almost a distant island.

The fans are alive. Giant red and black flags are everywhere; shouting and singing are the order of the day, large drums pound continuously. It's loud, raucous, and invigorating.

Suddenly from a small tunnel the players emerge onto the pitch and the crowd goes wild. Red and black balloons appear, fireworks explode, the screaming intensifies. You can see, hear, touch, and smell the excitement. No one is sitting, many are jumping up and down.

By the time half-time arrives I'm nearly drained. The day is warm so I grab a can of guarana; a soft drink made from guarana berries and high in caffeine. It's a popular drink in Brazil, reported to cure anything and everything, and has a great berry taste. It reminds me a little bit of cranberries. Not only that, it's made by our friends at Antarctica.

The second half ends with Flamengo winning easily. I'm exhausted but Eduardo and the other fans seem no worse for the wear. The Brazilians seem to be able to concentrate their fun and excitement. Ordinary life is laid back and relaxed, but soccer is an intense, serious business.

As for me, I'm tired and hungry, and I could stand a big plate of feijoada with a side of chicken hearts.

SWITZERLAND

Chapter 8

NO COUNTRY FOR
AN OLD MAN

SWITZERLAND

NOTHING BEATS the feeling you get from finishing an IRON-MAN® Triathlon. It has been one of the longest days of your life but also one of the very best days of your life. You've had a year's worth of pain and suffering crammed into a single brutal day that seemed like it would never end. Fortunately the long hours of training paid off and everything worked according to plan. The feeling of relief is profound, no more worries, no more living under the gun; you are delighted to be done.

I know that's how I feel. I've seen the bright lights, I've reached the mountain top, I've been to the Promised Land. The usual words seem insufficient and inadequate to describe the experience. I'm riding high, grasping at every metaphor in sight, tossing clichés left and right.

When I talk to normal people about the race, I do my best not to sound like a complete idiot. It was a long row to hoe, I tell them, definitely not a walk in the park. It was no piece of cake, I had to stay focused and I had to avoid spinning my wheels (except during the bike, of course). By the time I got to the finish line, I realized I was out of the woods and was ready to call it a day.

The clichés seem to go on forever but unfortunately that's not the case for the post- race euphoria. The excitement surrounding an IRON-MAN® race has a half-life of about two weeks. In the days immediately after the race, you get the chance to relive the event with your fellow competitors. Everyone did the same race, of course, but perceptions often differ. Some people were bothered by the hill that you barely noticed while the headwind on the bike that nearly stood you up was just a mild breeze to other athletes. Some thought the swim course was a little long, others aren't sure. No race detail is too small to ignore. This is a big event and it needs to be thoroughly dissected and analyzed.

Race expectations can vary greatly from athlete to athlete but anyone who completes an IRONMAN Triathlon is usually genuinely happy. It's a great achievement no matter what the finish time. Even the Big Guys who came up a little short are glad to get another notch on their belt. Their sub 10 hours may have turned into 11 hours but it's still a finish and there's a lot to be said for surviving a bad day. In IRONMAN racing, unexpected events are the norm and it's very tempting to drop out when things go wrong, so any finish is noteworthy.

For me, there is some solace in knowing that I tackled the same challenges as the Big Guys, there's a tremendous sense of community and shared experience. Some of it is glory by association, but there's also a bond based on respect. The waves were just as big, the hills just as steep, the miles just as endless. True, I may have spent seven hours on the bike while others barely needed four hours, but in my mind that makes my effort even more special.

The return flight home after an IRONMAN® race is usually a pleasant affair. There are lingering aches and pains but absolutely no anxiety. The spirit-sapping trials and tribulations of modern air travel are much less annoying on the return trip. I have plenty of time to chat with other athletes heading back to the U.S. My tall tales become a little more polished with practice, I add an extra dash of courage and never hesitate to exaggerate. That horrible episode where the airline lost my bike and nearly sent me to a mental institution is just a distant memory. I know that I won't need my bike anytime soon, the airlines can do anything they wish with my machine. I'm coming home. It's the return of the triathlon king.

■ ■ ■

Back at my house I'm not exactly a king. I'm more of a stranger. I become reacquainted with my family, the people I used to spend a lot of time with before I got into this deranged project. I start to bone up on the basics of my former life. Who is that couple that lives next door? When did you say our son graduates? What's our dog's name? These are small steps on the road to healthy, sane living.

Over a period of time, things begin to return to normal. I no longer view free time as a kind of provocation. There are long conversations, leisurely meals, hours spent doing nothing and everything. From my family's point of view, it's like I've just been released from prison and have returned home after a long period in the slammer. There's no post-triathlon halfway house, though, I've been dumped back into the regular world, cold turkey. My wife has to get used to me being around the house on the weekend. Sometimes I'm still in bed when the sun rises, I can even stay awake to watch *Saturday Night Live*. I know I'm a different man; I'm someone who only wants society to give him a second chance in life. My family is careful, they are living on pins and needles. I'm like a recovering alcoholic; I could fall off the wagon at any time.

Still, everyone is kind and considerate. They know that finishing an IRONMAN® Triathlon is important to me, so they act like it's important to them. For my family, there's an underlying question that lies unspoken, unresolved. "Why at your age did you do such a foolish thing?"

It's much too sensitive a subject to be broached head on, so they ask less threatening, more concrete questions. "How far did you say that swim was?" "Did you see any sharks?" "Do they have Gatorade in Brazil?" "Does your butt get sore from sitting on that bike for seven hours?"

Back at work, I'm a welcome sight. For months I've been slipping away early from the office, trying to squeeze in that extra swim or run. Some mornings I would show up late, still drenched with sweat, trying to adhere to my Spartan training schedule. I compiled a horrible work record. If there was any serious task to be done, I was usually nowhere to be found. I was the weak link in the work cycle for so long that my partners quit speaking to me. They're now ready for me to start doing my share.

Many of the people I see in my practice are my age or older. I've known them for years and they are friends as well as patients. By and large, they are bemused and befuddled by my IRONMAN journey. There's no real purpose or logic to the adventure. Most have worked all their lives and feel like they've earned the right to take it easy. One 80-year-old lady summed it up nicely when she volunteered, "There's no fool like an old fool."

My triathlon friends are a little more generous, they have a better sense of appreciation of what I have accomplished. I am very happy to get the opportunity to describe every part of my IRONMAN Triathlon in great detail. I've got a captive, informed audience and I'm not about to let them get away. There is absolutely no modesty on my part. When I tell the story, the wind is a little stronger, the hills a little steeper, the temperature much warmer. No one expects an ordinary, mundane experience. Heroism is the order of the day.

In fact, my story begins to sound like a tale straight out of Homer's *Odyssey*. There's a clash of titans, a battle with the fates, superhuman struggles. Not only that, I get to play the role of both Homer and Odysseus. I not only tell the story, I'm the hero of the tale.

After a while, it all wears a little thin. My triathlon family is not quite as enthralled as I hoped. They no longer believe me, they mistake my hyperbole for a pack of lies. No one sees me as Odysseus, instead I'm more of a geriatric Don Quixote.

All the questions, all the interest, all the excitement comes in the first couple of weeks after the race and then it all pretty well stops. The rest of the world goes about its business. My IRONMAN® experience was just a mere blip on everyone else's screen. It was a long hard day, but just that, only one day. Much of what I'm doing now seems small and insignificant compared to an IRONMAN Triathlon. I had a big goal that dominated my life for several months, and I finally reached it. What comes next?

Now that I don't have to train like a madman, I have an extra 15 to 20 hours a week. I try to use this extra time in a productive way, but sometimes I meander and wander. I have more time available but I seem to do less, boredom and purposelessness are all too common.

All this is fine and dandy. I'm making the post-race letdown sound like a major psychiatric disorder, a step on the road to a full mental breakdown. In reality it's just a normal slump that many people experience after achieving a major goal. It's like graduating from college, getting married, or changing jobs. This event is just another mile post on the road of life.

This all sounds pretty obvious but nothing is simple in the world of IRONMAN racing. Believe it or not, there's an impressive name for this less than impressive problem. It's called the Post-Triathlon Depressive

Syndrome (PTDS), a splendid name worthy of twenty-first-century soci-ety. Once you've identified and named a disorder, it's time to treat it. The answer is the PTDS recovery plan. Those very same folks who brought you these detailed mind-numbing training plans for the full distance triathlon—the very same people who rode herd over your mileage, the same crowd who closely monitored your heart rate, caloric intake, and sleep patterns—they all want to be of further assistance. You made it through the race, now it's time to enroll in the PTDS recovery plan. The plan has carefully calculated doses of stretching, light exercise, mental push-ups, and such. Follow this regimen and in no time at all you'll be well and fit, ready to re-enter the normal world.

I'm sure this is good advice, but I've got a much better idea for treat-ing the PTDS that's guaranteed to work. My plan does cost a little more, and it does require a good bit of time, but hey, that's what life is for.

My answer for the PTDS is simple: I've entered the 2005 IRONMAN Switzerland. I don't have time to get depressed, I've got to get to work training. I can hear Switzerland calling like a siren and I'm all ears. (The sirens in Switzerland actually prefer to yodel.)

I'm totally committed to the Switzerland race but my wife and family are less than thrilled. It's like I've volunteered to return to Vietnam or I've joined the Peace Corp or decided to go on the road with the Lawrence Welk Orchestra. "Another IRONMAN race?" they ask. "What are you trying to prove? We're sick of this stupid exercise stuff. Why don't you do something normal?"

"I was hoping all of you would come with me," I reply. "It'll be a great trip. We'll do lots of sightseeing and plenty of shopping. Besides, I know you all love Swiss chocolate."

Now they change their tune. "That's a great idea," they reply. "Staying healthy is important. All this working out helps keep you in great shape. We can't wait, when do we leave?"

My sons fall victim to work and family conflicts, but my wife Polly and my daughter Patricia are willing accomplices on the trip to Switzerland. These ladies can provide enough raw shopping power to keep the Swiss economy afloat for years.

I know I'll miss my boys, but at least I've got an outside chance of returning from this trip financially solvent. Five travelers in Switzerland would have meant near certain bankruptcy, a true budgetary black hole.

■ ■ ■

We arrive in Zurich early one July morning, exhausted from the overnight flight. Getting from small town Mississippi to big town Switzerland isn't simple. The three of us have fought delays, re-bookings, crushed legs, and bad airline food. Plus we've had to keep an eye on the packed bike case. It's always lingering in the background, creating confusion, annoying airline agents, taking up space, causing numerous problems and delays. It's like going on vacation with your lawnmower.

At our hotel we're greeted by a tall, lanky guy with long red hair pinned back in a ponytail. He looks like a leftover from the Woodstock generation, a man fast-forwarded from the 1960s. He's Ken Glah, one of the legends of the IRONMAN® world. His company, Endurance Sports Travel (EST), is responsible for all our travel details in Switzerland.

Ken lopes around answering questions, checking details, giving instructions to his staff, moving adroitly from one problem to another. His clients are the athletes and their families, here for the IRONMAN race. He seems like the ringmaster directing all the action, keeping the show going. Ken probably feels that zookeeper would be a more accurate description of his job, it's frantic and unpredictable.

Ken is in his late forties and he has carved a nice niche in the triathlon business. EST is prepared to take care of all your needs; they do everything but run the race for you. Air travel and accommodations are things any travel agent can handle, but Ken puts it all together in a complete package, tailored for the bizarre demands of the IRONMAN world. He's kind of a philosopher-king who manages to see the whole picture.

People participating in an IRONMAN® Triathlon are a little different, a little peculiar. Ken understands this, he has a bemused tolerance for misfits, he knows what you're worried about. You don't have to explain or apologize for wanting to eat breakfast at 4:00 a.m. on race morning. Ken makes sure the hotel restaurant is serving at that hour. If you make it back to the hotel after midnight, too exhausted to move, EST will usually have something for you to eat. Ken treats everyone with equal courtesy: IRONMAN veterans who have seen it all many times as well as newcomers like me who are still afraid of their own shadow.

Most everyone doing the race stays at the same hotel and eats together. This is great group therapy. Commiserating with your fellow athletes, you find out that you're not imagining things; you have a real solid basis for your anxiety and insecurity.

■ ■ ■

The morning of an IRONMAN Triathlon is always a time of great apprehension. I spend my time before the race in my usual way, questioning my judgment and common sense. What if I bomb out? What if I crash? What if I die? What am I doing here in Switzerland? Why didn't I just take my family to the beach?

On race morning, I'm up around 4:00 a.m. after a few hours of restless sleep. There are two alarms set to ring as well as a hotel wake-up call but I'm out of bed before any go off. Are these alarms really necessary? Has anyone ever overslept on race morning and missed the start? I'm sure it has happened somewhere to somebody, but I know it'll never happen to me.

After a quick breakfast with the mandatory two cups of coffee, it's time for the bus ride to the transition area. What a solemn procession of long-faced athletes. Everyone is overloaded with bags of gear and plenty of doubt and anxiety. No one laughs, no one even smiles. The dawn patrol is silent. It's like we're all catching a shuttle to our own funeral.

It's a dark, quiet Sunday morning in Zurich, and no one else is stirring. No one anywhere else in the world in their right mind stirs before dawn on Sunday morning. If there ever was a time I should be in bed, this is it.

Instead I'm in the transition area checking and rechecking. I went over my bike with a fine-tooth comb yesterday before I left it in transition, but it's time to look at it once again. How many times can I pump my tires, try the brakes, check the gear shifters? Does a machine have feelings and emotions? Should I lean over and hug and kiss my bike so it'll know I'm really counting on it? That would be a little strange, even for an IRONMAN® athlete, so I look for other things to do.

During all the pre-race preparations, the dawn gradually breaks, almost unnoticed. It's a warm summer morning, still and quiet, not unlike daybreak in the Deep South. In reality it's not exactly warm, it's more of what I'd call hot. This weather isn't what I thought I'd find in Switzerland. I expected chilly mornings, mild days, men in short pants bringing the cows in for milking. I wonder why I'm not out fishing, or maybe reading the morning paper on the patio, or even better, slumbering in bed. Isn't there an age limit on poor judgment? Aren't you supposed to get wiser when you get older?

As the starting time approaches, I'm standing patiently on a rocky beach, maybe 10 yards deep, with 1,200 or so other athletes, overcooking in my wetsuit. This rubber outfit has me simmering in the heat. There's no need to warm up, I need to get in the water and cool down.

Just a few minutes before the gun, the noise level rises. Everyone is moving and talking, checking their swim cap and goggles. There's background music plus a lot of announcements coming over the public address system. The music is in English, the announcements in German.

Then it happens, the magical sound, the call to duty.

Helicopters are heard overhead, one of the most exciting noises in the world, synonymous with energy and motion. Whop-whop-whop, what someone once called the sound of air being beaten into submission.

For many people, old songs often trigger memories, recollections of past events, trips back in time. It's much the same for me with helicopters. The noise reminds me of the year I spent as a flight surgeon in Vietnam. The rhythmic beating was a constant background sound at Da Nang, present during the day and night, remorselessly ubiquitous, competing with the roar of F-4 Phantoms taking off. When you're young, noise is energizing. As you grow older, you value silence. In some Vietnam veterans the sound of a helicopter can trigger bad memories, even Post-Traumatic Stress Disorder in a few cases, but for me the memories are mostly positive.

The helicopters circle, the gun goes off, and I plunge into Lake Zurich. This is probably the best place I've ever swam in a triathlon. The water is cool and clear, there are no waves, the buoys are big and easy to see.

The swim course is two loops, but you never come out of the water until the end. The route meanders through a pleasure boat harbor and includes a short trip around a man-made island.

I'm out of the water in 1:28, much better than I had hoped for and much faster than I have ever done in the pool. Unfortunately, I give a lot of the time back trying to get out of my wetsuit. Stripping off your wetsuit is a simple activity for most people but for me it's a big chore. Whatever agility and flexibility I had in my younger years are long gone. I feel like I'm Houdini trying to escape from the Chinese Water Torture Cell.

The bike course has three loops with each leg featuring several good climbs. It's one of those courses where the hills have descriptive names, like The Beast or Heartbreak Hill. This should always be a big warning sign to any cyclist. If a climb has a special name it has got to be tough. The easy ones rarely get named. You never hear of a hill called Baby Boy or Piece of Cake or Weenie Hill. It's always something sinister sounding, a bad omen for old legs.

The first loop goes quickly. I'm feeling good from my Johnny Weissmuller–like swim. The Beast, as its name suggests, is a beast of a climb but I make it. Heartbreak Hill comes somewhere around mile 33 of each loop, just 4 miles or so from the end, and is the steepest climb on the course. It's a narrow road, only a half mile long, packed with spectators. The crowd is everywhere, there's barely enough room to ride single file up the hill. There is a lot of noise, every other person is ringing a cowbell. The energy of the spectators seems to carry you to the top.

It is much warmer by the time I get my second shot at the Beast. I'm breathing a lot harder, sweating profusely, moving slowly. It's no longer much fun, the thrill and excitement are gone. When I reach the top I stop and rummage around for my electrolyte tablets. I've somehow managed to lose them along the way. On this second loop the Big Guys start to pass me like I'm a sick cow. The descent off the Beast is very fast but they fly by in droves. Either they're getting a lot faster or I'm really slowing down.

The second trip up Heartbreak Hill is hard, a nice crowd remains but nothing like the first time. It takes a huge effort to reach the top. My legs are dead. I've got forty miles to go and they're screaming for relief.

On the third and final lap of the bike, the temperature gauge on my bike reads 89°F, and I can definitely feel the heat. I'm barely able to make it up the Beast. My bike swerves back and forth across the road, I have trouble going in a straight line. The seemingly endless climb squeezes the sweat out of me. I'm going so slow that I expect to keel over at any time. Some little kids on the side of the road point at me and laugh. They're waiting for me to collapse and expire.

I've bonked. I'm absolutely drained of energy, every pedal stroke is torture. Sadly, I know what's happening. Like anyone who has ever done long bike rides, I've been there before. When you bonk, there's not much you can do but push the fluids and calories and hope you start to feel a little better.

The long descent into town does nothing to help me recover. The forty-five mile-per-hour speed that comes with no effort doesn't even frighten me this time. I'm too tired to be scared.

Back in town, about six miles from the finish, I'm ready to tackle the final trip up Heartbreak Hill. The bonk is so deep that I have to stop along the street, get off my bike, and sit under a shade tree in someone's front yard. I munch a PowerBar® and debate whether I should continue or call it a day. An elderly lady comes out of the house and asks me a couple of questions in German. When I sit there dopey-looking and don't respond, she says, "I veel call the doktor."

That gets me back up on my bike and headed toward Heartbreak Hill. If they gave an award for the slowest ascent of Heartbreak Hill, I would certainly have won. I didn't get off and walk my bike but I came awfully close.

From the bottom of Heartbreak Hill to the transition area is just a few miles, and I'm out on the run at around nine hours, about the same time as in Brazil. My "fast" swim time made up for my slow bike, but I'm still bonked, it's still hot, and I've still got a full marathon ahead of me. I have trouble changing my shoes, I have trouble standing up straight. I start out of transition still wearing my bike helmet and gloves before realizing my mistake.

The run course is flat and consists of four loops along the lake front. There's a little shade but the temperature is still in the high 80s and it won't get dark and begin to cool down until around 9:00 p.m. I manage to run only one hundred yards or so before I begin to walk. It's a feeble effort, but it's the best I can manage.

Time passes in slow motion. Pain is followed by more pain, torture leads to more torture. I see my family and get words of encouragement. I can see on their faces they have some serious doubts. They wonder if their breadwinner has gone off the deep end.

I'm wearing a race number with my first name printed in large letters across the face, along with USA. I attract lots of words of encouragement from the spectators. The crowd has a natural empathy for the slow guy, for the old guy, for the man who looks like he is about to die. I fit nicely in all three categories.

"Come on, John, just a little further," they yell. They don't realize I'm on lap two, not lap four. "Go John, go USA," "Hop, hop John, go George Bush."

When you're exhausted, being called by your first name is more of an irritant than a boost. You can't slow down, people are watching you. It's an unwelcomed accountability, like someone is there, checking on you, making sure you don't goof off.

Six-and-a-half hours after I began the run, I finally finish. It's been a tough experience. I tell my marathon running buddies to remember how bad they felt at mile 25 of their last race, to recall how much pain they felt near the end. This was my lot for the entire 26 miles, every single step hurt, no relief at any time.

I do somehow manage to run down the finish chute, trying my best to look composed. It's 10:30 at night and the Swiss spectators are loaded. Many have been drinking all day and they've packed the finish line area. People are grabbing me, slapping me, hitting me with those inflatable noise makers. Everyone on Heartbreak Hill earlier in the day must have loaded up their beer coolers and moved to the finish line. They're three sheets to the wind, but they're excited. The weak link has survived, the lowest common denominator has made it home.

In the post-race tent, I collapse on a floor mat, lie there a while, and give thanks that I'm done. I'm like an elderly mule who has been flogged a time too many, everything hurts, nothing works. I get someone to help me back up off the floor and I sit at a table and drink a couple of mugs of beer. It's a tepid brew that tastes like dishwater. More importantly, it does nothing for my aches and pains. A fellow finisher breaks the bad news, this is nonalcoholic beer, compliments of one of the race sponsors.

This has to be one of the worst ideas ever foisted on the public, a genuine crime against humanity. I can't believe the quality-conscious Swiss are part of this sham. I can guarantee the finish line crowd wasn't drinking this stuff.

What's next, low-calorie chocolate? Cows without bells? Swiss cheese without holes?

This race was a close call. I was just a few steps from ignominy and shame. Most of the races staged in Europe have an 11:00 p.m. cut off, rather than midnight. I had only 30 minutes or so to spare, but I made it. I gather my family and my bike, neither is allowed in the recovery area, and head home on the bus. It's a great ride, everyone is hurting, everyone is relieved, everyone is happy.

It's celebration time.

· · ·

Traveling around Switzerland is simple and easy. It's a small country, not even as big as the state of Mississippi, but Switzerland has a lot of stuff the people of Mississippi can only dream about.

There are all kinds of mountains, plenty of fresh clean air, lots of chalets, secret bank accounts, a huge number of cows and cowbells, many types of cheese (known collectively throughout the world as "Swiss cheese"), and beer with and without alcohol. Most of these things (except for beer) are hard to find in Mississippi.

One of the things I like best about Switzerland is the generous assortment of red Swiss Army pocket knives. You see them at every shop in the country, they are almost as common as postcards. What a weapon, they come with a variety of options. Corkscrews, can opener, scissors, bottle opener, screwdriver, toothpick. They even make them with a laser pointer and an MP3 player. If warfare ever reverts to knife fighting alone, the advantage must go to the Swiss Army.

Mountains are another thing that comes to mind when you think of Switzerland. Everyone, of course, has heard of the Alps (the varsity mountain range), but the Jura (the junior varsity mountain range) provides plenty of sightseeing opportunities as well. More than two-thirds of the country's surface is covered by mountains and the Swiss have figured out how to carry you to the top of the peaks. Swiss engineers have created a vast network of funiculars, cable cars, and cog railways to help you reach the summit. The trips aren't cheap, but they're well worth the price.

Polly and Patricia are full of energy and ready to see Switzerland. They already know the shops of Zurich's Bahnhoffstrasse like the back of their hand and they have developed a passion for chocolate that exceeds my devotion to IRONMAN® racing. The great city churches, the Grossmünster and Fraumünster are like old friends; they have managed to see every stained glass window in town.

Zurich is a great city. There are enough private banks and brand-name boutiques to service every rich person in the world, but we don't qualify so it's time to move on. Besides, this run-up to the race is not what they advertise in travel brochures. The ladies have had enough of hearing me moan and groan about the race, and they know that a real Swiss vacation doesn't begin at 4:00 a.m. and end at 1:00 a.m. the following day. They are certain that there's more to life than an IRONMAN Triathlon.

It's interesting; everyone has different needs and desires, and different family dynamics. IRONMAN families tend to be either supporters or tolerators. Some athletes bring along spouses who worship at the altar of their success. It's like their man has just whipped the world, his achievement has been their fulfillment. The IRONMAN Triathlon is the focus of the trip, they're along in a supporting role.

Not my family. They are very happy for my achievement, but they know that open roads lie ahead, a real holiday for the entire family. As for me, I've finished the race and all my body parts still work, so my kind and generous personality rises to the surface. I've had enough of this monastic IRONMAN regimen, I'm ready to see Switzerland.

We are on the go early in the day headed from Zurich to the Appenzell. This is the traditional Swiss countryside in all its splendid glory. There are none of the big city trappings you find in Zurich or Geneva: no overpriced jewelry shops, no teeming throngs of tourists, no streetcars overloaded with commuters.

In this part of Switzerland, everything is pristine and perfect. It's real life imitating a picture postcard. The mountains, the meadows, the contented cows, the colorfully painted houses, the traditional music (including great yodeling), the old-fashioned costumes, the locally made cheese and beer: Old Switzerland is alive and well in the twenty-first century in the Appenzell.

The Appenzell is also a great hiking area that attracts lots of tourists. Mt. Santis is nearby and is advertised as providing a "sweeping view of six countries."

In my experience, views of distant countries or states from the top of a peak are sometimes a bit of a disappointment. You see one giant distant horizon where the sky and land merge but there are no convenient lines, like you have on a map, to separate one country from another. It's a great view, but where does Liechtenstein end and Austria begin? You could be seeing three countries, or maybe five or six. It is a nice panorama, but it all looks the same.

Still, six at one time is hard to beat, so we decide to take the cable car to the summit. Unfortunately when we reach the top the whole area is fogged in. We can't see six countries. We can barely see six feet in front of us. It's a little better than being in a shower at home, but not by much. Still, I'm not complaining at all. This turns out to be our only bad mountaintop trip during our entire Swiss journey.

It is very pleasant to spend the day in the town of Appenzell. The local houses are distinctive with colorfully painted facades and attached barns. The small Church of St. Mauritius, barely mentioned in the guide books, has a beautiful Baroque interior. We enjoy a delicious lunch, sampling as many local specialties as possible, lingering on an outdoor terrace enjoying the view.

Appenzell is a small town, around 5,000 people, and after lunch we wander around the narrow streets, basking in the ambiance of the old town. We're soon attracted by the sounds of a large crowd coming from the direction of the town center.

This is great, maybe we'll get a chance to see the local Swiss citizenry, dressed in their quaint, embroidered costumes, meeting in open-air assembly. Or perhaps it's a local crafts fair, our opportunity to see those ancient skills passed through many generations. Or it could even be a traditional Swiss music festival, something I know we would all enjoy.

The three of us follow the noise, round the corner and discover the unexpected. There it is, right smack in the middle of Old Switzerland—beach volleyball. The whole town square is covered with trucked in sand, the nets are up, the bleachers are full, the crowds are whooping it up.

The guys on the court, barefooted in swim trunks, look like they have been shipped in from Santa Monica. It's what you'd least expect, Southern California comes to Switzerland. Travel is always full of surprises.

■ ■ ■

A good beach volleyball game is hard to top, but the next day the three of us head to the town of St. Gallen to visit the magnificent Baroque cathedral and the Abbey Library. These UNESCO world heritage sites are stunning, so rich, so ornate. Nothing is understated, the splendor jumps out immediately.

The library has over 150,000 books and documents, many over 1,000 years old. It's in the rococo style, sort of a Baroque gone wild. I know just a bit about the Baroque, and I'm generously available to share it with my family. I know that my little bit of knowledge is a dangerous thing, but that doesn't keep me from waxing eloquently about the features of the Baroque to Polly and Patricia. I share detail after detail, tossing in a few Latin words for good measure. I feel like I'm on a roll. I'm a born again tour guide, ready to proclaim the good news.

They are impressed with the church but they are not impressed with my unsolicited lecture services. Soon the ladies take to calling me "Professor Baroque." "You're right, Professor Baroque," they say, "that is a beautiful ceiling." "My goodness, what an ornate altar, Professor Baroque. Please tell us more."

This isn't the first or the last Baroque church we run across in Switzerland, so my title sticks for the entire trip. I may be a professor but I've got a bad group of students, inattentive, disrespectful, unappreciative. I deem them "The Incorrigibles."

A few days later we're in Lucerne, one of Switzerland's loveliest cities. The city's most famous landmark, the old covered Chapel Bridge, is found on every picture postcard of Lucerne. Much of the bridge burned in 1993, possibly from a careless cigarette, and had to be replaced. A real tragedy, this has to be one of the best reasons ever to not smoke: avoid burning down 600-year-old historic bridges.

A visit to the Old Town is followed by a walk through the Wine Market, a trip to the Lion Monument, and then a cruise on Lake Lucerne.

I won't pass up my special field of cultural expertise, so I head to the Jesuit Church. It's everything a student of Baroque could ever want. My girls want nothing to do with it, they've been Baroqued to death. While I look inside they go and hunt for more chocolate.

One day we take the cog railway to the top of Mount Pilatus. It's the steepest railroad of this type in the world, something we are reminded of at least a dozen times on our trip.

This peak is named after Pontius Pilate, and his spirit is said to still haunt the mountain. We're vigilant, spirits and ghosts can ruin a holiday, but fortunately we run into nothing worse than a high school group from New Jersey.

Mount Pilatus is just the beginning of our Alpine adventure, a week split between Interlaken and Zermatt lets us see many of Switzerland's most famous mountains. It's a different type of holiday: no museums, no shopping, just the breathtaking Swiss scenery. Each day seems to surpass the previous day, we soon run out of adjectives to describe the experience.

It's a short trip from Lucerne to Interlaken, the gateway to the Bernese Oberland. Every morning the three of us enjoy breakfast while gazing out at the magnificent view of the Eiger, the Mönch, and the Jungfrau. This is what makes a holiday a holiday. You are light years away from the stresses of ordinary life, each day begins on a positive note, a time for reflection and thanks.

One day we take a scenic ride to Mürren for lunch before ascending the Schilthorn; another day we have a pleasant hike to Grindelwald. The mountains actually soften everyone's temperament: we all speak a little gentler, no one argues or yells, everyone looks on in awe. It's a humbling experience.

Early one morning we board the Jungfrau railway for a trip to the Top of Europe. Our destination, the Jungfraujoch at 11,388 feet, is the highest railway station in Europe. Along the way, we see numerous signs and receive several verbal warnings, all carrying the same message: keep your arms inside the windows of the train. The route is narrow and tortuous, with many rocks, trees, and tunnel walls waiting to whack you when you least expect it. A danger only for the imprudent and the careless.

There are quite a few other Americans in our rail car, and we all talk about our trip, the things we love about Switzerland, what makes it a great country, what the U.S. could learn from the Swiss.

Everyone agrees there's a lot to admire. The Swiss love land, nature, and tradition. They are thrifty and industrious, you never hear of a prodigal Swiss. Cleanliness and punctuality are so engrained that they must be part of the Swiss DNA.

When we reach the Top of Europe we find glaciers, skiing, ice caves, ice sculptures—the whole winter panoply in the middle of July. The Jungfraujoch complex is packed with tourists, I never knew so many people could fit on a mountaintop.

The run over to Zermatt takes most of a day but we're in no hurry. Train travel in the Swiss Alps is a treat, not a chore. Some people pay big money to take day long train trips just to look at the scenery.

The small mountain village of Zermatt is tucked away in a deep valley dominated by the majestic Matterhorn. This is Switzerland's most famous peak. If the Swiss needed an official mountain, the Matterhorn would be the one. Each year, more than 3,000 alpinists climb the Matterhorn, more than the rest of the Swiss summits combined.

Zermatt is an idyllic place, reachable only by train. Transportation around town is mostly on foot, although a few electric vehicles and horse-drawn cabs are allowed.

Patricia and I spend a full day hiking to the top of the Klein Matterhorn and enjoy probably the best view of the entire trip. It's a little harder than we thought so the next day we opt for the rack railway to reach the Gornergrat.

There are a couple of St. Bernard dogs at the mountain top, available for photo opportunities for eager tourists like us. These dogs are lovable and adorable and we are all smitten. We may forget these strange sounding German names attached to all these Swiss mountains, but we won't forget the St. Bernards. When push comes to shove, it's hard to beat a good dog.

■ ■ ■

After spending our entire trip on the German-speaking areas of the country, the three of us head to Geneva, the largest city in French speaking Switzerland.

Geneva is a beautiful city, nestled in a little nook, nearly surrounded by France, fronting on Lake Geneva. The waterfront with its *jet d'eau* and quaint lake steamers attracts thousands of visitors.

This is a global city, a worldwide center of diplomacy. The United Nations, the International Red Cross, the World Health Organization, and many other agencies have a big presence in Geneva. There's a bureaucrat on every corner, the cost of living is out of sight.

The Geneva Conventions, dealing with humanitarian rules in wartime, were signed here. The city prides itself on being a neutral ground for dealing with many of mankind's biggest problems, and it promotes itself as the Peace Capital.

I'm happy to be in a place where I can talk to people, ask questions, read the signs. Everyone I meet in Geneva is pleasant and polite and on the move, most seem to be from somewhere else.

My group leaves no stone unturned in our exploration of Geneva. We feel like we've done justice to the mountains, and we don't want to shortchange Switzerland's second largest city.

We get frisked and photographed before touring the United Nations. It's the old League of Nations building and is much more beautiful than the UN headquarters in New York. Next comes the nearby Red Cross museum. I never realized this organization did so many different things in so many places.

One afternoon we wander through the old town and visit the Cathedral of St. Pierre. This is John Calvin's church and it pays homage to his Protestant God. You can still see Calvin's chair, almost 500 years old and no worse for the wear.

After such an adventurous trip, heading home is a difficult chore. Switzerland is a wonderful country—the picturesque mountains and countryside, the clean and efficient cities, the sturdy and industrious citizenry. I'm glad I came to this beautiful place.

Chapter 9

HURRICANES AND HIP FRACTURES

I'M FINALLY back home in Mississippi. Just a few weeks have passed since my trip to Switzerland, and I haven't even bothered to unpack my bicycle. My bike case is stuck in the corner of my storeroom, a forgotten reminder of my titanic struggle in the mountains. Switzerland seems like a distant, yet pleasant, dream. The country floats in and out of my mind. I can still see myself struggling across the finish line to the drunken acclaim of the Swiss citizenry. It never fails, memories improve with time, the pain and suffering disappear while the high points grow and endure. I find myself yearning for that clean, cool Swiss air; I'm ready once again to pedal effortlessly to the top of the mountain.

My friends have no interest in my IRONMAN® stories; they heard enough the first go round. Everyone listens politely but I can detect an undercurrent of poorly disguised indifference. Mentally and physically, I'm at a low point; no one is paying the least bit of attention to me. My motivation is nowhere to be found, I'm suffering in the brutal August heat, wishing that fall would hurry up and arrive.

Then, one Monday morning, Hurricane Katrina strikes and things change in a big way. The minor annoyances of life, the things that mean next to nothing, are gone. They're replaced by major problems. In just one day, my life is reduced to the basics—food, water, and shelter—everything else becomes superfluous, meaningless, unimportant.

■ ■ ■

Hattiesburg, my hometown, is located about seventy miles from the Mississippi Gulf Coast. It's a small town in a convenient spot; New Orleans, Mobile, and Jackson are within 100 miles. Hattiesburg is a college town, home of the University of Southern Mississippi, with a large medical community and a fairly stable economy. As the Chamber of Commerce likes to say, it's a great place to live, work, and raise a family. Life moves at a good pace, but you still feel like you're in control of your time and energy. People are friendly and polite, as interested in you as you want them to be.

Unfortunately, Hattiesburg is also located in an area prone to hurricanes. Unlike the coastal areas, there's little danger from flooding this far inland, but hurricane force winds and secondary tornadoes can wreak havoc during any storm.

A pattern seemed to develop here in Hattiesburg. Every few summers a new hurricane would threaten South Mississippi. Many times the storm would turn away from our coastline at the last moment and strike some less fortunate area. We would all watch the poor souls in Florida or Texas digging out of the rubble and would breathe a sigh of relief, thinking "thank goodness this one missed us." A few weeks later we would already have forgotten the name of the hurricane. It's hard to remember something that didn't directly harm you.

As the years passed, the hurricane warnings in my area produced an almost routine response, these were habits polished by the passage of time. Hurricane preparation was a ritual that everyone, to varying degrees, engaged in.

For several days we would track the storm, watching the weather bulletins, speculating on the direction and intensity, hauling out old hurricane tales, hoping the little red icon would weaken or turn away. If things continued to look bad a day or two before the projected landfall, there would be a big rush to Walmart to stock up on water, food, batteries, and other supplies. The shelves would be stripped bare as if a swarm of locusts had struck the store. Long lines would form at all the gas stations as some of the more prudent prepared to evacuate. A few industrious, well-prepared citizens would break out their gasoline-powered generators that had been in storage since the last storm threat.

The highways from the Gulf Coast and New Orleans would have bumper to bumper traffic as residents fled town. Local motels and storm shelters would fill with people escaping the hurricane.

Then the winds would hit Hattiesburg. If it was a bad storm, we would lose power for a day or two, a few streets would get blocked by falling trees or debris, some signs or awnings would bounce along the pavement. Local television reporters would stand bravely in the fierce winds, relaying reports back to the main studio

Over the decades, the hurricane threat in Hattiesburg was less than impressive for most of us. We would miss a few days of work, but in a week or so everything would be back to normal and everyone would begin looking forward to the important things in life, like the beginning of the school year and college football season.

Storm survivors, like military generals, are almost always reliving the last great battle, preparing for the past. My hurricane battles had all been small ones. I had been underwhelmed by the whole experience, and I had become very complacent. My memory, like the rest of my body and soul, had weakened with time. I no longer went to Walmart for supplies. I didn't get in line to fill up my vehicle, I didn't even worry. On the inside, I used to laugh at those people who ran around like busy ants, preparing for a storm that never arrived. I was a real life grasshopper, looking forward to the rain and wind and a break in the summer heat.

Sometimes ignorance isn't bliss.

■ ■ ■

Hurricane Katrina arrives in Hattiesburg late one morning bearing sustained winds of 100 miles per hour. The storm starts in the Bahamas, later crossing the southern tip of Florida before entering the Gulf and intensifying. It crosses the southern tip of Louisiana before making final landfall near the town of Bay St. Louis, Mississippi.

Over the weekend, I watch the storm develop with a mixture of annoyance and excitement. It's like watching a NASCAR race, most of it is boring and repetitive but there is always a chance that a big crash will occur. There's a type of perverse allure in waiting for the twisted and bloody wreckage that might come.

I'm at home around nine o'clock in the morning when the wind and rain pick up. Soon the debris begins to fall and in just a few minutes the power goes out at my house. I'm stuck with no computer, barely enough light to read, and a home that is more than a little stuffy. These are the danger signs of incipient boredom. I'm nothing if not resourceful, so I jump in my car and drive to my office a few miles away. We have underground utilities there, so I should be able to work without problems until the pesky storm passes.

On the way over, I find that the wind is stronger than I expected and

I have to make a couple of detours to avoid fallen trees. Still, I remind myself that this is much better than sitting around at home with nothing to do.

I'm at my office all alone for maybe 15 minutes before the power crashes. I sit there for the next three hours while the wind blows and blows. It dawns on me a few hours into the storm that I should be concerned about Polly and John, who are still at home. By this time the phones are down, and there is no response on the land lines or the cell phone. So, I sit there in the dark and wonder why I do such stupid things. Why don't I think ahead? Why don't I realize that, just because something has never happened before doesn't mean it would never happen?

The 100 miles per hour winds feel, sound, and look bad. My office shivers and shakes, the noise is like a truck motor, as limbs and other debris blow by. The rain comes in great horizontal sheets. I'm not smart enough to move to the interior of the building or to lie on the floor or cover myself with a mattress or cushion. (This is standard storm survival advice, repeated dozens of times each hurricane season.) Instead, I just sit and look out the window for two to three hours. I'm still not totally sold, this is a little more than I expected, but I'm hoping it will be over soon.

Around 2:00 p.m., the wind lightens and I head outside to take a look around before driving home to check on my family. It looks like a bad scene from a horrible disaster movie. Fallen pine trees are scattered about like broken matchsticks. Some are lying flat, others half broken, others leaning precariously. Massive trees that have survived decades are sheared to pieces in seconds.

These beautiful trees have created an obstacle course, a gauntlet to run as I make my way home. The roads are free of traffic, not even a police car or emergency vehicle is about. The entire front of one business has collapsed, leaving it open to the world like a dollhouse. I turn down one street but I find it blocked by a downed power line so I have to back track. Most of the other routes also have fallen trees across the roads. I'm forced into detour after detour, sometimes driving into people's yards in order to skirt by fallen trees. Eventually I make it to within a half mile of my home before abandoning my car to hike in.

It is not a welcome sight. Three giant trees have fallen onto my house, crashing into one of the bedrooms. My son John is at home and had just managed to get out of the way.

John, Polly, and I are relieved to see each other; we have all imagined the worst. The car ride home has left me stunned, this was a terrible storm. I'm left with a healthy respect for forces bigger than I am.

If you watch television, this is the time in the natural disaster story when a distraught survivor appears on camera and says something like, "Thank God no one is hurt, I've got my loved ones, all of this can be replaced." That is not me. I never suspected my family would be hurt so I'm not so much relieved as I am crushed. The monster pine trees in my bedroom have done nothing to improve my disposition. I want my house back.

I am a slow learner, but I eventually realize that I'm more fortunate (or less cursed) than a lot of people who endured this hurricane. In my county, seven people died as a result of the storm; in Mississippi the number is more than 235, while overall the toll is nearly 2,000. My home is simply damaged, while most buildings along the Gulf Coast are completely destroyed. In New Orleans, the floods are just as devastating. Everyone I know and love is alive and well; for many others the survival of friends and family is in question.

By late afternoon the wind and rain have mostly died off, and the three of us go outside to survey the damage. We are all numb, sort of in a trance, too drained to say much of anything. A few neighbors are milling about, but no one has escaped damage. Roofs are torn asunder, trees block the roads, and many houses are crushed.

Katrina seems to have thumbed her nose at storm preparations. Those with foresight, those who did their best to prepare for the hurricane, those who played by the rules sometimes fared worse than the lackadaisical disorganized souls like me.

Katrina leaves me full of self-pity, I'm cursing my bad luck, feeling very sorry for myself, when I get a lucky break. Cell phone service is practically nonexistent after the storm, but somehow I get a call through to my friend and contractor, Brian. He is in his home outside of town, blocked in by fallen trees, but he promises to come check my home the following day.

This is great, I have hit the jackpot. After a hurricane, a good repairman is priceless. Everyone has problems, everyone needs help, and I have found a good man whom I can trust. Most people are forced to wait weeks for home repairs.

My friend Brian shows up the morning after the storm and starts to work on the pine trees in my house. I'm very appreciative. I give him praise, water, food, money, anything he wants or needs that I can provide. Three days later, the cut trees are stacked at the curb and my roof is covered with a huge blue tarpaulin.

South Mississippi turns into a blue tarp wonderland. They are everywhere, dotting the rooftops, giving a checkerboard flavor to the skyline. For many years to come the blue tarps would be a universal ornament, a colorful reminder of Katrina's power.

For the next couple of weeks, life is reduced to bare essentials: ice, water, and food. There is no power, no air conditioning, no running water, no working toilets, no telephone, no computer. The heat is oppressive; it's like spending every moment of your life in a sauna or steam room. Sometimes I move a mattress outside to sleep, but it remains overbearingly warm, even at night. Pretty soon, I start to smell bad, like most everyone else. It's a lingering funky odor that intensifies as the days progress. I miss my running water.

There is one place that is almost like heaven, a true sanctuary from the heat. That is the inside of my car. My favorite pastime consists of driving around the neighborhood in air- conditioned comfort, checking out the hurricane damage, listening to soft music. Sometimes I almost forget how bad things are.

For me, a typical day consists of rising at dawn, eating some horrible-tasting canned food topped off with warm, bottled water, working like a dog in the hot sun, complaining to everyone who will listen, dreaming of taking a shower, then finally falling asleep not long after sundown.

For the first time in many years, the need to exercise never enters my mind. I'm working out, but it isn't running, swimming, or biking, it's basic manual labor. I'm hot and sweaty, my muscles and joints ache constantly. At the end of each day I feel like I've finished a marathon.

Around ten days out, I get together with a couple of my running buddies for a short jog. We take turns leading each on various routes designed to show the hurricane damage. One street takes us past a house where three crushed cars remained wedged in a collapsed garage, another turn leads us to a home where you can look through the front of the house all the way to the backyard. The house has literally been chopped in two. Each one of us tries to outdo the other; it is a sad, pathetic form of entertainment.

My bike survives the hurricane, just missing a crush from a fallen carport beam. The roads aren't clear enough to ride safely for many weeks. Swimming pools are among the last sites to reopen. This isn't a time for triathlon, it's a time to survive and rebuild, a time to give thanks and look to a better future.

The Katrina recovery does wonders for me. I've always leaned toward the easy side and I'm shamed and inspired by watching other people giving up their time to help those less fortunate. There's a lot to do in life. These people could have stayed at home and tended to their own needs. I'm not a cynic, I'm not even a skeptic, but I do need to be reminded from time to time of the inherent goodness of human beings.

. . .

Most bad things fade with time and it's the same with Katrina. We all live in the present and look toward the future. Yesterday's problems are soon replaced by fresher challenges.

By late October the heat has vanished. Most of the roads are clear, the mountains of debris that once lined the edges of the streets have been carted off to landfills. There are big empty spaces where there used to be trees and buildings. Most of the repairs on my home are completed. My new roof blends in nicely with all the other new ones. I'm ahead of many people; there are still a lot of blue tarps in town, indicating work to be done.

As summer slowly fades into autumn, the Longleaf Trace, our local rails-to-trails project, is finally clear of debris, and I start back riding a bit. The trail is 41 miles long and heavily wooded, so it takes longer than expected for the crews to finish the job.

Thanksgiving weekend rolls around, just three months post-Katrina. It's one of those picture-perfect times that pop up frequently in Mississippi in the fall. My family is at home, the food is delicious, the weather is gorgeous—this is a time to be thankful.

I'm out one afternoon with our local bike group, finishing a pleasant 40 mile ride. There are a dozen or so riders and we are only one mile from the finish. Everyone is cooling down, talking back and forth, about to wrap things up. We're riding probably 15 or 16 miles per hour, slightly disorganized, but nothing intense.

I'm talking, laughing, not paying close attention to the other riders. Then it happens, my front wheel hits the rear wheel of the biker in front of me and I go down.

"Here we go again," I think, in that fraction of a second between bike contact and ground contact. I've had maybe three other falls in my brief cycling career and I know they're no fun.

It never fails, the ground hurts like hell. When you're in your sixties, everything is painful. I could fall on one of those special mattresses they show on television and not even knock over the glass of red wine at the other end yet still manage to injure myself. When you're young and you fall, you bounce; when you're old and you fall, you break.

My left elbow is cut pretty good and my left hip and shoulder are bruised and sore.

My first big thought is: "I've just thrown $1,000 out the window." I haven't met a dime of my health insurance deductible for the year and I know the emergency room will have the meter running from the moment I hit the door. My $1,000 will be swallowed up by the ER in no time at all.

I start to ride the last mile to the finish and then drive myself to the ER, but one of my friends insists on taking me. Everyone is treating me just like you would treat a little old lady who has stumbled crossing the street.

During the ride to the hospital I mull things over, cursing the trenchant unfairness of life. After a bicycle accident I always feel like a fool and an idiot.

I'll admit I'm a bigger dunce than most cyclists, but my story isn't unique. Anyone who has ridden a bike for any length of time at all has a crash story. I've seen two friends and neighbors killed in bicycle accidents in my lifetime, and I've read of dozens of others. Unfortunately, it's not an uncommon story.

I pummel myself mercilessly all the way to the hospital, now it's the ER's turn.

Emergency rooms are designed to pile frustration and delay on top of pain and suffering. I muddle through the long waits and the trip to the x-ray department. The ER physician turns out to be Patrick, the little kid my son's age who grew up across the street from me. My hip, shoulder, and elbow all hurt, but not too badly. I'm ready to get sutured up so I can go home and brood some more.

I'm sitting patiently in the ER trauma room, wondering what I'll eat for supper that evening, when in walks my new best friend, Dr. Con.

Dr. Con is a tall, lanky, middle-aged man from New Jersey. His travels brought him to Hattiesburg to practice hand surgery but he's the orthopedic surgeon on call and he has to take care of anything that comes in off the street, even geriatric bicyclists.

He brings good news; my shoulder is fine, just a bruise, it should heal with time. He also brings bad news: my hip is broken. I have an open comminuted elbow fracture. I'll need two separate surgeries. I'll have to spend at least five days in the hospital.

Dr. Con doesn't really use the good news/bad news bit; he is delivering all bad tidings. He starts by telling me all the complications that are looming in the background—loss of elbow function, osteomyelitis, avascular necrosis of the hip with hip replacement surgery. There are a lot of bad things out there, and they are all waiting to strike me. He even points out, by golly, that people die from this surgery.

Ho-ho-ho, Merry Christmas to you too, Dr. Con. The official Christmas shopping season has just begun, and I may not ever see it end. By the time Santa arrives I may be dead. My family and my bicycle could be in deep mourning.

■ ■ ■

This whole business is a big change for me. Practically all my life, I've been the physician, I've hardly ever had to play the role of the patient. This is my first major surgery, my first real stay in the hospital. I have spent my entire professional life acting like I knew what I'm doing and getting away with it. Now I'm on the receiving end. It's amazing what you notice from the other side of the fence. Little things that never register when you're a physician are big deals when you are the patient. Small kindnesses and benign oversights are magnified many times over.

This is my first ever general anesthesia. I've operated on thousands of patients in my lifetime, usually using a local anesthetic, but sometimes employing a general. It's still an eye-opener; one minute I'm talking to my wife in the pre-op area, seemingly a brief moment later I'm awake in the recovery room. Dr. Con uses his drills, hammers, and chisels for several hours, but I never know it.

After surgery, I don't have to worry about getting up to go to the bathroom anymore. When I awake in the recovery room, I see that I'm sporting a brand new shiny urinary catheter. A giant orange tube snakes from my most precious private part down to a bag of amber fluid hanging on my bedside, a true surprise.

Obviously this isn't all that great, but surprisingly it really isn't all that bad either. Since I have an open fracture, I'm receiving $20,000 worth of intravenous antibiotics (I check the hospital bill when I get home), and this keeps me from picking up a urinary tract infection. I think Dr. Con forgets that I have a catheter, so I enjoy the privilege of the house for a full three days.

Instead of lying in bed needing to take a leak, I lie in bed and hurt like hell. I do have a patient-controlled analgesia (PCA) pump, one of modern medicine's great achievements. This little gadget gives me an instant intravenous hit of pain medicine whenever I push a button. I could have used one of these when I was climbing Heartbreak Hill in Switzerland. In theory, it works great, better pain relief with less medicine. In reality, I get the entry level PCA pump when I need the deluxe, supercharged model. My thumb is sore from pressing the button. I hurt a lot more after the surgery than I did before. Dr. Con tells me I have a bad injury, and that I should be glad that he did everything he could to fix it.

This whole bicycle accident is a giant nightmare—multiple surgeries, near constant pain, ugly tubes sticking in and out of my body, hardly any sleep. However, there is one beneficial result, one unexpected consequence that makes it almost worthwhile. Dr. Con and I become close, personal friends.

Dr. Con is an orthopedic surgeon, and according to the Hippocratic Oath, he is limited to a maximum of one minute with each patient when making rounds. Dr. Con soon starts spending one minute and thirty seconds, sometimes even two minutes, with me on his daily visit. We laugh, we joke, we remember those old medical school days.

The bond strengthens.

Many people don't realize that being a physician is a lot like being in a college fraternity. You have all your fellow brothers to pal around with and share the good times.

Throughout my recovery, Dr. Con, my close friend and brother, orders plenty of x-rays. The Hippocratic Oath also requires at least one x-ray per day when hospitalized. Dr. Con has done one hell of a job, and he wants to make sure that nothing comes undone. These giant pins in my hip and these wires and plates in my elbow could slip out of place in an instant.

Sometimes we talk about my fractured bones. Of course, I don't call them the "hip bone" or the "elbow bone," I use the real names, the femur and the olecranon. The hardest part of becoming a physician is learning the fancy names for everything. With patients you can use whatever name comes to mind ("Madam, you have an acetabulum in your eye"), but with fellow physicians you need to be a little more precise. The more of these big words you can string together, the better it sounds. I'm not sure if Dr. Con is impressed or not. He leaves the room before I can find out.

■ ■ ■

At day five I'm finally able to go home. It's great to shower and shave. There are no mirrors in the hospital. I stare at my bathroom mirror and a skid row derelict looks back. You can't really get clean in a hospital. Everything about me has the smell of death; I look like someone has fished me out of the gutter.

My family treats me like a king, they bring me anything I want. I lie in bed for hours reading but after a while I get bored. A weak mind like mine can absorb only so much of the written word at one time.

Life turns into an endless procession of hollow days. I fire up the television and start watching CNBC, the business channel. The stock numbers are so repetitious that they nearly put me to sleep. I channel surf, taking in everything the medium has to offer. Daytime television is often dismissed as pathetic and trivial, but that is an understatement, it's really a lot worse than that. It's death by a thousand soap operas, game shows, and talk shows.

I shouldn't have worried; salvation is really just around the corner. At day seven, I notice I can stand up and walk around without too much pain. At day eight, I drive to my office and check my mail, at day nine I ride the stationary bike for thirty minutes. Life is looking a lot better since I got out of the hospital.

At day 14, I go back to work and start back swimming, and at day 21, I jog a mile at the track.

Although there's no extra credit for getting well quickly, I'm just happy to be able to exercise. The combination of injury and age can be an irreversible liability. I never knew how it would all turn out.

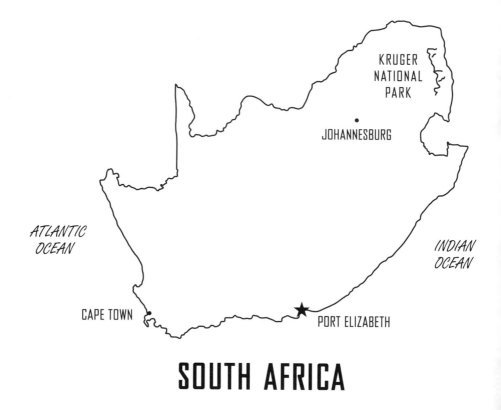

SOUTH AFRICA

Chapter 10

BACK ON THE ROAD

SOUTH AFRICA

MY BROKEN bones have mended and I'm back to swimming, biking, and running. I give thanks every day for the fact that I'm still able to work out. I know that a hip fracture can be the beginning of the end, a terminal event for someone my age. Still, I have to face reality, I'm not the man I used to be.

Since I've started back running, I'm a good minute per mile slower. It's all a little perplexing, because everything feels the same as before. I'm still stiff and sore when I start, an hour run still feels like an hour run, this much effort still produces that much shortness of breath. Nothing seems all that different, it's just that my stopwatch reads a minute per mile slower than it did last year. Sometimes I wonder if I should buy a new watch.

I am already pretty slow so I don't have a lot of cushion in my run time. In fact, I am quickly becoming a permanent fixture in the back of the pack, a man whose arrival heralds the end of the race.

I draw on clever strategies derived from the wisdom of my years to fight this drop in performance. First, I double up on my vitamins (if only life were this simple), then I buy a new pair of running shoes, then I train a little harder, then something starts to hurt and I'm forced to take time off to recover. I re-calibrate my goals and go about my business; my mind quits making commitments that my body can't keep. Reality has a way of tempering expectations: you are what you are.

I can't complain, though. The two years following my bike accident are not bad at all. I get more and more accustomed to being slow. Small accomplishments take on a greater significance than before. There are no big goals, just small victories, little steps that go unnoticed by everyone else.

I do some local triathlons, plus I throw in an occasional big trip. No great challenges, but enough to keep me active and moving.

Back home, my age group begins to thin out a little. Some guys get tired of the challenge of training, some pick up a bad knee or hip or back or a similar ailment. It's a never-ending battle, the aches and pains of a vintage body.

Still, a few rewards remain for those who muddle along. One of the advantages of getting old is that you garner great praise for insignificant achievements. It doesn't take a lot to stand out in the crowd of seniors.

■ ■ ■

A week before Thanksgiving, my ship comes in. I've hit the jackpot, I've won the lottery, I'm a made man.

Not quite, but almost. Ken Glah, the owner of Endurance Sports Travel, calls to tell me that I've won an expense-paid trip to the upcoming 2008 IRONMAN® South Africa. I had registered several months back for the great giveaway that included airfare, hotel, and race entry fee. Ken's daughter pulled my name out of the hat, somehow managing to avoid several thousand better qualified triathletes.

I'm elated. All my life I've been entering contests and this is the first time I've ever won anything of value. I've been chasing something-for-nothing since the day I was born. Up until now, I've only been pursuing a dream; now I'm a winner.

I'm excited to win this trip to South Africa. It's not just the money. More important, this stroke of good luck validates my strange triathlon habit. When someone asks, "Why do you still do that exercise stuff at your age?" I reply, "Oh, haven't you heard? I won a trip to the 2008 IRONMAN® South Africa, all expenses paid." Here's the best part: many of them think I won the trip based on a sterling athletic performance. They don't know it's the luck of the draw. Tiger Woods "won" a trip to the Masters and I "won" a trip to the 2008 IRONMAN South Africa. We're both winners in my book.

This is great timing. For the last few months I had been mulling over another IRONMAN trip, checking out the various travel possibilities. It's good news at a good time. I've got about four months to go until race day.

■ ■ ■

In preparation for South Africa, I do a quick and honest evaluation of my fitness and conditioning. Two years have passed since I last trained for an IRONMAN Triathlon. It's a mixed bag, at best. My biking and running are slow, I'm way short of the miles I need, but it is a cold time of year, and I feel like I can put in the training to bring them up to a decent level.

Swimming is a big problem. I haven't spent much time in the pool, and it shows. I'm so slow that I feel there is a serious chance I might miss the two hour, twenty minute cutoff time. I'll be swimming in the Indian Ocean and last year's race had high winds and big waves. I need to be able to survive a bad day at sea.

My mind conjures up a horrible scenario: I train all winter and tell everyone about the trip to South Africa, but then I miss the swim cutoff and must return home to spend the rest of my adult life explaining why I never even made it to the bike, much less the run.

This whole swimming game is strange, it's a fragile thing in the best of times. I'm sure I'll know how to run and ride a bike until the day I die, but I can't say the same for swimming. I feel like I've never owned my swim stroke outright; I've merely leased it and it's under a constant threat of repossession. If I miss more than a few days in the pool, someone from the sheriff's department with a gun on his hip will knock on my door with foreclosure papers, and I'll be underwater in a big way.

Fortunately, the fitness center where I swim has recruited a swimming instructor; this may be just the thing I need. I've never had any lessons, so my potential may be untapped. I could be a precious stone waiting to be polished and brought to perfection . . . or more accurately, a dying ember hoping to be coaxed back to life. In any case, maybe I can get a little better and make the swim cutoff time.

Kasey is the lady who can unlock my hidden talents. She is tall and slim with a dark, exotic beauty, sort of like a young Penelope Cruz. She is just a few years out from swimming competitively in college, and her form in the pool is nearly perfect. I've never seen swimming look so effortless.

Kasey watches me swim a few laps and is a little taken aback. This may be the biggest challenge she's ever faced. She tells me that I've got a lot of strikes against me—bad form, bad habits, bad heart and lungs. (Kasey says all this in a nice way, but I can read between the lines. She's looking for a way to send me to the arthritis pool.)

I'm persistent, though. I tell her there's practically no downside. She can't lose, the only way I can go is up. Kasey is young, good-hearted, and she needs the money, so she signs me up.

These lessons are a new experience, and I find them interesting, nothing like I imagined they would be. I go once a week for an hour or so. Kasey is polite and encouraging. She says "do this" and I do it, she says "hold your arm this way, rotate like this, kick like that." I'm like a sheep dog following his master's commands. I respond to straightforward instruction, recognition, and praise. Kasey gives me detailed workouts for other days (in my mind I call these plans "recipes for success," but I don't say that out loud. I always try to appear mature and sophisticated in front of women).

I follow these recipes religiously (Betty Crocker would be proud) for about six weeks, but absolutely nothing changes. My times remain slow, and I'm starting to lose faith. Maybe past a certain age swim lessons no longer work, maybe the ingredients in this recipe are too old. Then one day, about eight weeks or so along the way, the coaching kicks in and I get a lot faster (a lot is a relative term). There's about a month until the race, so this works out well. I'm happy, and I can tell Kasey is glad to turn her attention to more promising clients.

Bike training means that it's once again time for those long Saturday morning rides. Since I've sworn off the indoor bike trainer, I spend a lot of time perched on my carbon fiber machine out in the cold. This is my first experience with cold weather riding, and it goes pretty well. Most days the temperature is in the thirties or forties, occasionally it drops into the twenties. I bundle up and enjoy the winter dawns. The trails are quiet and deserted, everyone else is at home in bed, meaning I can ride for hours in peace.

Running remains a major chore. Stiff joints and weak muscles are my constant companions, but the workouts are much more tolerable in the cold than in the heat.

Everyone says that the time spent training is more important than the speed or distance. I'm not sure I believe that, but I hope that it's true.

■ ■ ■

I've recruited my daughter Patricia to go with me to South Africa (or maybe she recruited herself. With your children, it's hard to know who is really in charge). I head to New York City to spend a few days with her, and then we gear up for the trip.

This is a beast of a flight. The seats are cramped, the movies are awful, and the food is even worse. The flight from New York to Johannesburg alone is eighteen hours. Our crew bails out about halfway at Dakar, Senegal, and another group carries us to Johannesburg.

Patricia and I spend just enough time in Johannesburg to rent a cell phone and eat an ostrich burger. These burgers are not unheard of in the United States, but they are a fast-food staple across South Africa.

Our race destination is Port Elizabeth, a city of around a million people in the Eastern Cape province of South Africa. You can't go much further south on the African continent without falling into the Indian Ocean.

I'm excited, I've been reading everything I can get my hands on about South Africa. I've got lions and elephants and Zulu warriors dancing in my head. This is a country I never thought I'd visit; it's as distant as a distant land can be.

Patricia and I are met at Port Elizabeth by our group leaders, Greg and Robin. This is probably the most relaxed, most enjoyable IRON-MAN® trip I've ever taken. There are around 1,400 entrants in the race, but most are from South Africa. Just a few dozen athletes are from the United States, and our travel group is small with only eight competitors plus assorted family members.

Strangely, there are four people from Mississippi entered in the race. Larry, George, and Stephanie are all from the Jackson area, and like me, this is their first trip to South Africa. Larry is a cardiovascular surgeon and George is an orthopedic surgeon. Both are from out of state but were recruited to the faculty of the medical school.

The star of our group is George's girlfriend, Stephanie. She is in her late thirties and has spent her entire life looking slim, fit, and attractive. This is her first IRONMAN Triathlon but we are sure she'll do well.

Greg, our tour leader, is a competitive cyclist, and he knows what we need and want. His girlfriend, Robin, has figured out how to drive on the left side of the road so she fills the role of chauffeur. The rest of us do our best not to get run over when we cross the street. Greg and Robin take us everywhere—registration, practice swims, bike rides, course tours, pre-race banquet, grocery shopping. We're all nervous and scared, but maybe a little less so than normal, thanks to our genial hosts.

. . .

The IRONMAN® South Africa race is held is held right smack in the middle of Nelson Mandela country. The swim takes place in Nelson Mandela Bay, the run course includes multiple loops through the Nelson Mandela Metropolitan University campus.

Besides its proud connection to Nelson Mandela, this area has another claim to fame: sharks. Locals boast that it hosts more different species of sharks than any other place in the world. During the practice swim, I actually saw a shark, about three or four feet long, cruising along the bottom. It wasn't huge, but it was big enough for me. I mentioned it to one of the life-guards but he told me not to worry. He said the small sharks aren't dangerous; you only need to worry if they are 5 feet or longer. Maybe I should carry a tape measure with me when I swim.

I'll have to hope someone else keeps the sharks occupied on race day, but I think I'll be pretty safe. I've always heard that when sharks select their prey, they prefer the tender flesh of the young and immature. If that's true, I've got nothing to worry about.

Our group is up at the usual 4:00 a.m. on race day. First comes breakfast and then a short drive to the transition area.

The swim is a two loop affair. You head straight out, turn left past a giant pier jutting out a hundred yards or so, then make a circle and head back home. Next is a run of a hundred yards on the beach before going back into the water for the final lap.

Fortunately, the Indian Ocean is fairly calm, and the sharks are conspicuous by their absence. I feel really comfortable, those swim lessons have paid off. I'm through the first loop in 43 minutes, wave at Patricia, stop to get my picture taken, and head back in for the second loop. I finish in 1:28, including the beach run—better than I had hoped for.

The three loop bike course includes a gradual six mile climb at the beginning of each circuit. Early in the first lap, my friend Skip catches me. He's from California and is an IRONMAN® veteran. I figure that if I can stick close to him, I'll be okay.

Skip is in his early forties and is a much better athlete than I'll ever be. I settle in three bike lengths behind him and put my mind on cruise control. There are a lot of race officials riding the course on motorcycles, so I'm careful to stay out of the draft zone. Skip makes it nice and easy, he sets the pace and I follow. If I catch myself getting too close, I ease back a bit. If I manage to get in the draft zone a time or two, I'm not too concerned. There are worse things that can happen in the world of triathlon, like getting eaten by a shark, for example.

I'm carrying several flasks full of energy gel and I suck the stuff down along with bananas, water, and Gatorade. We're through the first lap in about 2:10 and I'm feeling surprisingly good. Skip is my *domestique,* leading me on, checking back from time to time, making sure I'm okay.

The climb on the second loop is not too bad. Skip and I laugh and talk and the miles go by quickly. The whole lap is maybe seven or eight minutes slower than the first. The final 15 miles or so of each lap run along the Indian Ocean, making for a magnificent ride. The rocky shore is lined with crashing breakers interspersed with beautiful coves and sandy beaches. The scenery in South Africa is definitely equal to the Alps, and the ride is a lot easier on the legs.

By the third lap, my *domestique* is gone. Skip has absconded up the road, and I'm forced to think and pedal at the same time. The six mile climb on my own is a lot harder. It's gotten hotter, and they seem to have steepened the roads since I was last here. Still it's tolerable, definitely no Heartbreak Hill. I get all the way to mile 95 before I begin my ritual of checking my odometer every fifty yards.

Just past the 100 mile mark, I'm suddenly struck by flavor fatigue. I've downed several flasks of raspberry energy gel with careless abandon, and now I'm sick as a dog. Each flask holds five servings, and I'm on my fourth packet. It's amazing, just a few miles back this stuff tasted great, now the gel is threatening to come up for air. I'm certain that I'll never want to taste another raspberry for as long as I live. My stomach feels like it's full of leftover ostrich burgers.

I stumble out of the second transition around 8:30, my best time yet, thanks in good part to Skip. I'm in good shape time-wise but in horrible shape health-wise. Giant waves of nausea are followed by dry heaves. I can't find my electrolyte tablets; I seem to have a talent for losing them. The folks in the changing tent have never heard of such a thing. I ask twice for electrolytes and they hand me a jar of Vaseline. A few sips of water are followed by gagging and heaving, I'm hoping all this will pass.

Early in the run, Patricia pops up alongside the road urging me on. She had watched the swim from start to finish, then left to visit some friends in Port Elizabeth, go to church, eat Sunday dinner, play with the friends' children, and still managed to get back in time to catch the whole marathon. This event is a long day for competitors and spectators alike. No one ever says, "I haven't gotten enough. I wish it was a little longer, I hate to see it end."

The run course is a three loop journey that includes a circuit through Nelson Mandela Metropolitan University. The crowds are big and noisy all along the way. There are a lot of roadside barbecues and some serious beer drinking. The barbecues, or *braais* as they are known in South Africa, seem to raise my nausea level a notch or two. They smell awful. There's a lot of back and forth chatter between spectators and participants, most of it in Afrikaans. I can't understand anything.

This is a bad situation, a nauseatingly unpleasant experience. I can't hold anything down. I know I need fluids but anytime I drink, I gag. I'm getting progressively slower as the hours pass. I'm not moving at much more than a slow walk, a shuffling gait of six inches or so. The suffering is slow, unrelenting, and undramatic. There's a sense of impending doom. On the last lap I'm swaying from side to side as I alternate walking and shuffling. I keep staggering along, looking like a drunk leaving a bar at closing time. A medical team tries to get me in a van but I've only got three miles to go and I'm determined to finish.

There's an old general surgery axiom you learn early in medical training: All bleeding stops. Similarly, all marathons end eventually. My 6:41 run puts me home at 15:15. It's an ignoble end to a difficult race.

As soon as I cross the finish line I head for the medical tent. I know I need help, I don't need to be convinced.

The first thing they do is put me on the scales. At race registration, everyone was weighed. My weight, eighty kilograms, was written on the back of my race number. My new post-race number is seventy-one kilograms. I've dropped nine kilograms, close to a twenty pound weight loss. I feel like a giant piece of human jerky.

Now, I know that some of the loss may be due to clothing and I realize that scales can differ, but still, that's a lot of pounds to leave on the roads of South Africa. Twenty pounds in one day—it's better than liposuction. Maybe I've discovered a new weight loss plan: 7 hours of exercise with no fluid tacked on to an 8 hour workout.

The medical tent looks a little like the battlefield scene from *Gone with the Wind*. There are stretchers full of beat-up bodies, sounds of moaning and groaning fill the air, and harried-looking medical personnel run amok. The nurses find a nice cot for me in the tent with the other ne'er-do-wells. I'm ready for some intravenous fluids, I'm certain that a couple of liters of fluids will pick me up in no time at all and return me to the land of the living.

For some reason, it doesn't work like that in South Africa. Instead, my physician, Dr. Johann (I call him Dr. J in a futile attempt to ingratiate myself) checks my electrolytes, gives me an intramuscular injection of Phenergan® (an anti-nausea drug), and hands me a bottle of Powerade®.

What's going on? I'm nauseated, I can't drink anything. I beg and plead for an IV. I use my most submissive, pitiable tone of voice (it's almost second nature after 40 years of marriage). I offer to pay for the IV fluids. Doesn't Dr. J know that I'm a fellow physician, a brother in the art of healing, a member in good standing of the medical fraternity?

Well, my medical fraternity must not have an international chapter because Dr. J isn't budging. He assures me I'll feel fine in just a little bit.

He even offers me a chicken sandwich from a big bag labeled CHICKEN KING.

I don't need fried chicken, I need fluids and the only way I'm going to get them is through mini-sips of Powerade. For the next couple of hours I lay on the cot wishing the Phenergan would kick in, hoping that I'll be around for the next African sunrise.

The medical tent is right next to the finish line, and I listen to the blaring music as the race announcer welcomes home each finisher. The official finish-line song of song of the 2008 IRONMAN® South Africa is "Y.M.C.A." by the Village People. It plays nearly continuously over night-club quality speakers until my ears want to bleed. The lyrics are beamed directly into my brain, a bold audio tattoo. I can't shake it.

I'm sick, everything aches. I'm dry as a bone, it seems like years since I took a leak, yet I'm very happy. I've finished, I know that sooner or later I'll quit hurting. It's a wonderful feeling, once again euphoria and relief, unrivaled anywhere in the world.

By dawn the next day I'm doing great, everywhere I look the sun is shining. When the breakfast buffet opens, I set a new South African record for the most orange juice drunk at a single setting. It tastes like the nectar of the gods, my body absolutely craves it.

Everyone is happy, everyone in our group finished the race. Stephanie turns out to be the fastest Mississippian and I turn out to be the slowest, no surprises there. It's all fun now, the hard work is behind us and Patricia and I are anxious to see South Africa.

■ ■ ■

Cape Town is probably the most beautiful city on the African continent. It's situated on a small peninsula jutting into the Atlantic Ocean at the southern tip of Africa. Patricia and I are eager tourists and we're ready to do our sightseeing duties. Cape Town is a melting pot of cultures. There are a tremendous number of blacks as well as whites, but there are also large numbers of Cape Coloureds. This latter category is a mixed race group of descendants of Dutch settlers, their slaves, and local indigenous people. Most are native Afrikaan speakers, and at various times over the years, they have received better treatment than blacks under apartheid. Under the apartheid system they occupied a middle land between black and white. Racial categories have been abolished in the new South Africa, but the Cape Coloureds have been slow to embrace the African National Congress, the ruling political party.

Cape Town sits at the foot of Table Mountain, an appropriately named flat-top mountain. It's part of a large national park that extends all the way down the Cape Peninsula to Cape Point. A popular spot, many think that Table Mountain is the most climbed massif in the world. It's not very crowded, but our time is short so we take the cable car to the top. The wind is ferocious, Cape Town is one of the windiest cities in the world. The sunset is burnt orange and beautiful, the city bowl sits in a dark shadow. It's beautiful in the extreme, we feel like we're looking at the bottom of the world.

One day we connect with our guide Faisal for a trip to the Cape Peninsula area. Faisal, a Cape Coloured Muslim in his forties, is one of the most intelligent people I've ever run across. He knows absolutely everything about South Africa—history, politics, sports, music, science, and so on.

As we head south down the Cape Peninsula, Faisal introduces us to the unique plant life of the area. He points out that there are only six plant kingdoms in the world and one of these, the Cape floral kingdom, is found here on the southern tip of Africa, occupying only 0.04% of the earth's land area. Much of this land is covered by a natural shrubland vegetation known as fynbos. You can find some nine thousand or so species and most are unique to the area. There are hundreds of proteas and ericas and other strange plants. If you like rare and unusual species, the Cape Peninsula is the place to go.

Faisal is a walking encyclopedia and he has a couple of avid listeners. Patricia and I ask a lot of questions, and this encourages Faisal to tell us more. The next day I find that my brain is overloaded with South African flora and fauna. I decide that the best way to clear my mind is a trip to the Cape Winelands.

We visit Stellenbosch, host to the country's leading Afrikaner university, then we continue on to Paarl, home of an Afrikaner memorial as well as the site of Mandela's long walk to freedom. The final stop is Franschhoek, the community founded by the French Huguenots.

It's no simple trip, we're stopping and tasting wines all along the way. Things are getting better and better. Everything is wonderful and the country is finally coming into vivid focus. I'm grateful someone else is driving.

■ ■ ■

Wherever you go in South Africa, people are eager to give you advice on what to do and what to see. It seems that everyone knows the ins and the outs of the entire country. Headed to Port Elizabeth, we hear, "it's a laid-back place, nice beaches, watch out for the sharks." Going to Cape Town, they say, "one of the most beautiful cities in the world, be sure to visit the top of Table Mountain and don't forget the wine country." Spending time at Kruger National Park, it's "try to see the Big Five animals."

For Johannesburg, it's different. The universal admonition is "watch out for the crime, muggings and car-jackings are common events, never go out alone, you might not make it back." It's not advice on what to see, it's advice on how to stay alive.

Johannesburg, the financial and commercial hub of South Africa, is the country's largest city. It's located on the Highveld, a mile-high plateau, and it got its start in the late 1800s as a gold mining city.

The contrasts in Johannesburg are striking. The northern suburbs are beautiful, wooded areas with lovely homes protected by high walls topped with razor wire. On the other hand, shanty towns, overcrowded and often lacking water and electricity, are sometimes just a few miles away from rich estates.

Everywhere we go in South Africa, Patricia and I do a lot of walking and talking. South Africans all seem eager to explain the journey from apartheid to a multiracial democracy. They've lived through a historical change and they are rightfully proud of their country. In Johannesburg, it's a different story. People seem a little more streetwise, a little more savvy, skeptical and suspicious. They give you a wary look when they talk to you.

We're booked in Sandton, one of the very nice leafy northern enclaves of Johannesburg. After repeated warnings, we stay pretty much in the commercial areas. There are the same clothing chains, fast-food outlets, and shoe stores that you see in the U.S. It's not much different than visiting a mall in Atlanta or Dallas. We're careful and cautious but we're not alone; even Nelson Mandela has moved north. We drive by his home in Houghton and see the same walls, barbed wire, and armed guards as everywhere else in town.

A guided tour to Soweto turns out to be full of surprises. This famous black township, part of the Johannesburg metropolis, was the seat of resistance to apartheid. The area was originally created to house black laborers who came from the countryside and neighboring countries to work in the mines. Soweto has all the expected problems—poor infrastructure, overcrowding, high unemployment, and crime. I've been to the favelas, the slums of Rio de Janiero, so I expected the usual tin roofs with no running water or electricity. There are plenty of these areas but there are also many middle-class areas with good homes, schools, and parks. There's even a convention center.

We drive down Vilakazi Street, a small road that once was the home of two men who would both later win the Nobel Peace Prize, Nelson Mandela and Bishop Desmond Tutu. Their former homes are modest dwellings but they definitely occupy the moral high ground.

■ ■ ■

When you think of South Africa, it isn't the typical tourist attractions that come to mind, it's wild animals. Patricia and I ride from Johannesburg to Kruger National Park with Jens, one of the Kruger guides. Once a month or so, Jens ferries a group of tourists from Kruger to Johannesburg, overnights with his family members in Johannesburg, then brings a new group of visitors back to Kruger. He enjoys catching up with his family, but he detests the city life. Jens is as close to the wild heart of life as a man can be. He sees Johannesburg as the dark side of South Africa, all of the country's worst features compressed into one place.

Jens is an Afrikaner and he loves his family, the outdoors, rugby, and beer. He's also a great guy. Jens answers every question we ask with, "for sure." For him, it's a verbal tick, a universal prefix and suffix.

"Jens, will we see a lot of elephants in Kruger?" "For sure, they're everywhere."

Jens, how long have you worked at Kruger?" "Ten years. It's a good job, for sure."

"Jens, tell me about rugby. It's not very popular at home." "For sure, I love the game."

I've pressed the right button. Jens spends the next thirty minutes explaining the details of rugby. Patricia is getting bored, I'm getting confused, and Jens is getting excited. It's hard to explain some things with words alone so Jens realizes that it's time for some hands-on coaching on the sport of rugby.

We stop at a rest stop and Jens demonstrates the dropkick technique, then he recruits some passersby and we lock arms for a maul or scrum, or something like that. Jens even attempts to show us how to leap high in the air to contest a line-out.

We talk at length about the great South African Rugby World Cup victory of 1995. This was the first major sporting event to take place in South Africa following the end of apartheid. Rugby is a white Afrikaner sport rarely watched by blacks, but the South African team, the Springboks, was warmly embraced by Nelson Mandela. The ultimate Springbok victory served as a form of racial reconciliation for the country.

Jens describes how he cried when Mandela, dressed in a Springbok jersey and cap, came onto the field to celebrate the South African championship. He confesses that this was a defining moment in his life, one that changed the way he views other races.

When we finally arrive at Kruger, I feel like I've had an intensive tutorial in rugby. My mind is loaded with rugby rules and facts, all of which seem to disappear by supper time.

Jens drops us off to his buddy Alfred, who serves as our guide for the next five days in Kruger. Alfred is a native Sotho, and is one of a growing number of blacks who have joined the middle class following the collapse of apartheid.

Kruger National Park is an amazing place. It's roughly the size of the state of Massachusetts and has more species of mammals than any other game reserve in Africa. Every National Geographic special you've ever watched seems to come to life in real time at Kruger.

We spend our nights in one of the camps, completely fenced in, inside the park. Our fences don't keep the animals in, they keep them out. No one wants to be devoured by a lion or trampled by an elephant while on vacation. We want to watch the game, but we're not ready to be eaten.

Twice a day, at dawn and in the late afternoon, we head out with Alfred in his truck to see and photograph the animals. We always hit the waterholes, a popular spot for viewing. All the animals seem to get along well when it's time to drink (sort of like humans).

It's an amazing experience to be bouncing along a dirt road and see a herd of elephants emerge from the bush to lumber across the way. These massive grey dreadnoughts are always impressive and watching them in the wild never gets old. In contrast to much of Africa, elephants have thrived in Kruger, and the park now has too many pachyderms. They've tried everything from birth control to relocation in an effort to manage the population.

Like every other visitor, we want to see and photograph the Big Five—elephants, rhinoceros, lions, leopards, and Cape buffalo. These are the elite of Africa, the most dangerous of the wild animals. Fairly early in our trip we manage to see them all, except the buffalo. Kruger has thousands of buffalo but the big herds have supposedly moved to another area.

Much of the fun of game watching is being the first in your group to spot the wild beast. Someone in the group sees an animal, then everything stops, whispers and hand signs take over, cameras come out, and everyone jockeys for position, straining to get the best view and the clearest photo.

So, we are all excited one day when Patricia says, "Stop, buffalo!" Alfred pulls up and we glance across the road. Number five on our Big Five list is coming right up. Unfortunately, it's not a buffalo, it's a wildebeest. It's big and brown and impressive in its own way, but it's not a Cape buffalo. We all laugh and from now on Alfred refers to every wildebeest we see as "Patricia's buffalo."

These wildebeest are common and they seem to pop out when you least expect it. However, compared to impala, wildebeest are extremely rare. There are probably 100,000 impala in Kruger National Park. They come inside our camp at night, groups of 20 or 30 seem to be hanging out around every bend in the park. They're as common as cows in Texas. We soon take to referring to Kruger as "Impala City."

It's a wonderful routine that never gets old, and I love every day of my visit to Kruger. We rise before dawn, bundle up to stay warm, spend three or four hours looking at the animals, then eat a midmorning breakfast overlooking a river full of hippos and crocodiles, take a midday nap, and repeat the game watching until dark.

We are impressed by it all—zebras, giraffes, baboons, rhinos, hippos, warthogs, elephants, lions, leopards. We have enough photos and memories to last a lifetime. It's difficult to return to the ordinary world after visiting such an extraordinary place.

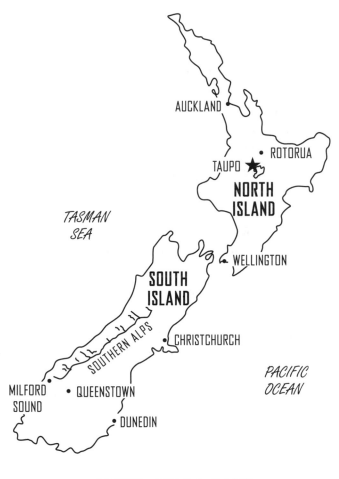

AUCKLAND

ROTORUA

TAUPO

NORTH ISLAND

TASMAN SEA

WELLINGTON

SOUTH ISLAND

SOUTHERN ALPS

CHRISTCHURCH

PACIFIC OCEAN

MILFORD SOUND

QUEENSTOWN

DUNEDIN

NEW ZEALAND

Chapter 11

A LAND OF GREAT SURPRISES

NEW ZEALAND

N EW ZEALAND is a different place.

For nearly all of its history, New Zealand has been a land without people.

The first humans to arrive were the Polynesian explorers who came in long canoes over vast distances. Their descendants are today's Maori.

The new arrivals found a strange land. Except for a few bats, there were no mammals. Instead, the visitors encountered giant flightless birds, some bigger than ostriches. The islands also contained bizarre reptiles and frogs, but fortunately no snakes (this makes my wife happy). There were thousands of plants and animals unknown anywhere else on earth. It was like the flora and fauna of New Zealand had evolved without reading the rule book.

The strange creatures lived in a world of dense forests, snowcapped mountains, volcanoes, geysers, and waterfalls.

The magic persists today. New Zealand has remained, above all, a place full of surprises.

This is my fourth IRONMAN® Triathlon. I've huffed and puffed, twisted and turned, trying to get a few more miles out of my worn out body. I'm ready to see New Zealand and meet the Kiwis. Everything I hear is good. They say if you don't like New Zealand, you don't like friendly people and natural beauty.

It's really impossible not to like the Kiwi nation. New Zealanders by and large are solid, practical, down-to-earth people. This is a land where strength, dependability, rugged independence, and above all, modesty are part of the national fiber. It's an easy place to be at home. New Zealanders believe their land is a special place and they cherish the simple outdoor life. This is not a country for flashy, big-shot types. Kiwi society is more egalitarian than most. There's an unspoken assumption that no person is better than any other.

The Kiwis value ingenuity; they believe they can solve any problem with whatever resources are available at the time. In New Zealand, it's called the "number 8 wire" mentality (number 8 fencing wire can be used to fix most anything that's broken). Kiwis are proud of their skill with animals and machines.

There is probably no better spot in the country for the IRONMAN New Zealand race than Taupo. It's a small town of just over twenty thousand people located at the center of the North Island, and it seems that practically the whole community has turned out to support the 25th anniversary of the race.

Since New Zealanders take every opportunity to head outdoors, Taupo is a popular holiday destination. The town is located on the banks of Lake Taupo, the country's largest lake; a lake so big that it has its own tides. This freshwater volcanic lake, known for its crystal clear, cool water, is a source of local pride. Everyone tells me it's clean and pure, ready to drink, no treatment necessary.

Taupo is a lovely site, the snowcapped peaks of Mt. Ruapehu and Mt. Tongariro loom in the background. There's boating, skiing, hiking, and climbing, not to mention superb trout fishing. (The region claims to be the trout fishing capital of the world. Several different species of trout were first brought to the country in the late 1800s by sport fisherman, including rainbow trout which came all the way from California.)

New Zealand was the second country to host an IRONMAN® Triathlon. The first race, of course, was held in Hawaii in 1978. By the early 1980s, the IRONMAN concept was beginning to take off. The event was on television, the number of entrants was increasing each year, and the potential for growth was obvious to everyone.

Hawaii is a long way from almost everywhere; it was time to give athletes in other parts of the world the chance to experience the pleasures of this event.

Around the same time that IRONMAN powers were considering expansion, the marketing experts at Air New Zealand were searching for a special event to draw travelers to their country. What could be more special than an IRONMAN Triathlon? The Kiwis are great sportsmen, they love a good challenge. It was a perfect match. IRONMAN New Zealand was born, the inaugural road show for the IRONMAN brand.

■ ■ ■

In Taupo, the wind almost always blows mightily. It whips and whirls, rising and falling, rarely stopping. In 2006, it reached near gale force and the water on Lake Taupo became so rough that the swim leg was cancelled and the IRONMAN Triathlon was reduced to an anemic duathlon, a mere 56 mile bike ride and a 13.1 mile run. In 2012, the race was postponed for a day (a true logistical nightmare) and staged at the half distance.

Luckily, when race day rolls around, the weather is in my favor. The wind is from the north but the water is perfect, crystal clear and cool. It's misty, foggy, and raining, a day without shadows. There'll be no over-heating today.

The swim is a straight shot, one loop down and back. The course parallels the shore line, maybe fifty to a hundred yards or so away from land, close enough to hear the spectators lining the lakeside.

It's great visibility, the other swimmers seem like synchronized automatons; they all move on the same beat, everyone appears to have great form. I'm swimming along comfortably when I encounter a totally unexpected marine creature. There are hundreds, maybe thousands, of these objects littering the bottom of the lake. Little, white, dimpled spheres, all the same size, just over an inch in diameter. Is this another oddball Kiwi trick of evolution? The answer proves to be much simpler, more twenty-first century. This bottom-dwelling organism is the New Zealand golf ball.

There's a floating golf green, moored off shore in 15 feet of water, just to my left. For a modest fee, golfers on the shoreline get the chance to hit their shot over the water and onto the green and hopefully into the hole. These duffers seem to be saddled with my golfing skills, the bottom of the lake is packed with poor golf shots. I swim a hundred yards past the floating green and continue to see golf balls.

I exit the swim in 1:32 and run a good quarter mile up a hill to the first transition area. A quarter mile isn't very far but it seems almost criminal to add this extra challenge to an already difficult task. My legs are hurting and I haven't even started the bike. This extra run could turn out to be the straw that breaks the camel's back (or even worse, it could be the *last* straw).

There are two loops on the bike with a group of hills at the beginning and again at three or four miles from the end of each circuit. Very quickly I'm out of the town and onto the flat farmland; a countryside of nothing but crops, cows, sheep, and wind.

Everyone is spread out; there are a lot of race officials out and about, and they look like men on a mission. There are no packs of riders today. The leaders pass me coming back, spread out in an echelon formation. They're all wearing Big Guy bike helmets and are stretched out on their aerobars, molded onto their machines. I clunk along, happy to reach the bike turnaround at the town of Reporoa and get the wind at my back.

The last few miles back into Taupo are a gradual downhill, so forgiving that a slow biker like me can cruise effortlessly into town at 25 miles per hour. The gentle slope gives an illusion of speed where none exists; it creates a sad emulation of vitality. At this point, it's raining heavily and I'm amazed to see the streets of Taupo lined two or three deep with cheering spectators. The umbrellas are out in force; the weather hasn't dampened the enthusiasm of the citizens of Taupo.

Whenever I see someone hanging around to cheer me on, I'm both surprised and grateful. I'm neither fast nor athletic but I enjoy playing the part. An unsolicited gesture of admiration or encouragement is always appreciated. In reality, this is more likely an act of charity; much like watching the school play of a neighborhood child, it seems like it should be acknowledged.

I'll have to admit that most of these spectators are waiting to see the Big Guys finish their second loop while I'm still on my first go-round. They're not exactly waiting for *me*, but that's okay, they are kind enough to yell words of encouragement.

The second bike loop is more of the same except that the hills are harder, the wind is stronger, and the spectators have all left to watch the professionals on the run.

I wander out of the second transition at around 8:43, happy to be done with the bike but dreading the twenty-six miles on foot.

This is the point in the race when I start to figure out how slow a running pace I can maintain while still finishing before the cutoff time. It's a useful mental exercise, it keeps me from thinking about how much I hurt and reassures me that I'll be able to finish. It's good for my brain and good for my soul and gives me hope to go with the pain. Still, it can also be discouraging. I've been through this before; I know the worst part of the race is yet to come. True bliss lies on the other side of the marathon, a good six hours away.

The marathon course heads from the center of town, alongside the shore of Lake Taupo to the local airport and then returns via the same route back into town. It's a two loop journey and the crowds are big, especially near the town center.

The shore of Lake Taupo is lined with parks, motels, homes, and a few apartment complexes. When heading out of town on the first loop, I notice an apartment building with a large hot tub out front. There are a handful of young women in bathing suits lounging about, laughing, drinking, enjoying the day, waiting for the lake sunset. The rain has stopped and the air is cool and fresh, it's a good time to enjoy the warm whirlpool. These ladies are happy and content, but I hardly give them a second thought. I'm trying to keep moving forward, struggling to maintain my dead man's shuffle.

The women are still there when I return on the first loop and again when I head out on the second loop. They wave and yell words of encouragement to everyone. I'm too tired to even acknowledge their greetings; I just push ahead to the last turnaround.

It's after 9:00 p.m. when I reach the twenty-three mile mark, just a little over three miles to go. I wonder if I can finish in less than 15 hours. I start calculating but I just can't do the numbers. I'm not even sure what kind of pace I'm running, each mile seems slower than the previous one. Plus, it's so dark I can't even read my watch, my vision seems to be failing like the rest of my body.

Besides, I tell myself, what does it matter, a finish is a finish. No one back home knows the difference between 14 hours or 15 hours. Not only do they not know, they probably don't care, either. I'm wallowing in self-pity and despair, a place I know all too well.

Around this time, I reach the apartment complex with the hot tub and notice that a couple of the young women are still there. One young bikini-clad gal sees me slogging along, springs out of the hot tub and runs in my direction, yelling, "She'll be right mate, you're doing great, keep it up, mate!"

She's thin and blond and I can see her freckles in the dark. She grabs me, wraps two arms around me and starts squeezing me and kissing me.

I've got neither the might nor the means to resist this unexpected, rather pleasant assault.

She stops and says, "Mate, you're almost there," a couple of more kisses then, "mate, you finish up and come back here. We've got this hot tub and some beer waiting for you."

I'm stunned and exhausted, nothing would suit me better than a beer and a visit to the hot tub, but I need to finish. After more than one hundred and thirty-seven miles I've only got three more to go. I manage to break loose, or rather my young lady friend pushes me in the right direction, and I'm on my way.

This whole episode is bizarre, surreal, and totally unanticipated. I wonder what's going on, or how I can explain this strange turn of events. After 14 hours, I know I look more shopworn and dim-witted than usual. How have I suddenly turned into a man that young women want to hug and kiss?

My mind mulls the possibilities. After all, I *am* an IRONMAN®, headed to my fourth finish. Maybe I proved to be irresistible to this woman. She watched athlete after athlete pass by and she saw one she just had to have.

This possibility is of course ridiculous. She could have enjoyed some serious hot tub time with any of a thousand other athletes who preceded me. That's crazy; it would be like passing up Brad Pitt to spend time with Grandpa Jones. Not likely.

The real answer is simple. I must have arrived about the same time the second or third six-pack of beer kicked in. These ladies have gotten cheerfully hammered. An alcoholic haze blurs the vision and softens the senses. If you have enough drinks, everyone looks alike.

After repulsing the bikini-clad young woman trying to take liberties with me, the last few miles prove to be manageable. I get to the one kilometer mark and take off running—no more of this sissy walking, no more complaining, the finish line is just ahead. The Kiwi nation will be waiting on the edge of their seats to see if I break 15 hours.

I'm across in 14:58 and I immediately sit down in the nearest chair and dry heave a couple of times. I would have been very happy with any finishing time under 17 hours. Cracking 15 hours is just icing on the cake.

This is the best I've felt after an IRONMAN® Triathlon. Some will say it's due to good fluid intake or perhaps better training, or maybe more experience.

As for me, I'm just glad to be done. I wonder how things are going back at the hot tub.

■ ■ ■

A couple of days later my body is still stiff and sore, but the race and hot tub memories are beginning to fade. I'm ready to hit the road to see the rest of New Zealand.

It's a short trip from Taupo to Rotorua, not much more than a half hour once someone points me in the right direction. Roturua is known for three things: geothermal activity, Maori culture, and tourists. It's a popular stop on most New Zealand holidays, a place where nature and natives come together in one package.

I can tell that I'm approaching Rotorua long before I arrive, I can smell it. The hydrogen sulfide odor of rotten eggs permeates everything, an unpleasant side effect of this geothermal wonderland.

Scattered around the area are boiling mud pools, some thick and black, others rusty brown and watery. You can hear them simmering, bubbling, gurgling from yards away. Hissing, spitting, and belching, they seem to have bubbled up from the deepest bowels of hell.

Geysers are the biggest draw; they shoot jets of water that head high and straight into the air before being blown off course by the wind. These eruptions are crowd pleasers; each one is greeted by "oohs" and "aahs" and gets captured by hundreds of cameras.

Almost as popular are the dazzling terraces of silica and other minerals that display a kaleidoscope of color, the pinks and blues are particularly stunning.

In the nineteenth century, Rotorua was a great spa town that drew tourists from far and wide. Many came to see the famous Pink and White terraces before they were obliterated by the 1886 eruption of nearby Mt. Tarawera. An elegant Tudor-style bath house set in the formal manicured Government Gardens remains today, a reminder of grander times. Once a great gathering place for the rich and famous, it's now a museum.

Rotorua is just one of many spots in New Zealand where the innards of the Earth seem ready to burst outward. The country is located on the Pacific Ring of Fire and it has seen more than its share of earthquakes and volcanic eruptions. As Johnny Cash knows too well, the Ring of Fire is a dangerous place, so I'm moving on to a safer spot.

I'm headed to the Agrodome. I'm a lucky man, there's no better place on the planet for an introduction to the Wonderful World of Sheep.

When I hear New Zealand, I think of sheep. This nation takes its sheep seriously. Every tourist guide book written reminds us that while the population of the country is barely four million, there are over 40 million sheep.

Nearly every tourist group that ventures into New Zealand is booked into the Agrodome. A lot of travelers are uncomfortable mingling with other tourists, they feel that this exposure to the masses somehow diminishes the travel experience. They want to spend their time only with the locals.

That doesn't bother me; I enjoy off-the-rack, mass tourism. Some of my best travel experiences have come from being herded around with a group of strangers. Besides, I'm a simple, uncomplicated fellow; I'm not at all embarrassed to lap up the standard tourist schlock. I like to learn new things and I'm not afraid to ask the dumb questions.

At the Agrodome, an eager audience sits comfortably in an arena as some nineteen different breeds of sheep are paraded, one at a time, onto the stage. They're introduced in much the same manner that you would introduce Miss America contestants.

"Here's the Merino, highly prized for its wool." "And now, New Zealand's dominant breed, the Romney." They're all beauties in their own way.

I never knew there were so many varieties of sheep. Some breeds are good for wool, some are better for producing lambs, some yield a lot of meat, some do better in dry climates; all are adept at taking a dump on stage while tourists take their photograph.

After the parade of beauties, one unsuspecting animal is brought on stage and shorn of his wool in just a minute or two. The shearer grabs the electric clippers and it's done before the audience has time to focus their cameras. It's like walking into a barber shop and coming out bald before the door has time to close. The naked sheep scampers away, apparently no worse for the experience and everyone applauds.

Later in the morning we watch the sheep dog trials. These are smart animals, they move the flock from one pen to another, reacting instantly, anticipating the movements of the sheep before they happen.

Sheep versus sheep dogs, it's not much of a match. The dogs have personality, panache, intelligence, and charm, while the sheep are timid, dim-witted, and docile, completely lacking in spunk and courage. The sheep look like they're going through the motions, punching the clock, waiting for a quitting time.

. . .

It's a short flight down from the Rotorua area to Christchurch, the largest city on the South Island. Every place in New Zealand seems to have either a British name or a Maori name, some have both. The English names—Wellington, Blenheim, Nelson, Canterbury, Palmerston, Marlborough—are a bit easier to remember and to pronounce. Visiting the country is like taking a refresher course in British history.

The Kiwis sometimes say that New Zealand is more English than England and this especially holds true for Christchurch. The British and the Irish were the early settlers of this country, and the link to the motherland has held strong throughout most of the twentieth century.

In Christchurch, you don't have to close your eyes to imagine that you are in England. The manicured civility of Britain is all around. There's punting on the Avon River, strolling through Hagley Park and the Botanic Gardens, watching the Christ's College boys headed to class in their black-and-white striped blazers, attending services at Christchurch Cathedral. There's enough of England to satisfy anyone's Anglophile itch. It's like Christchurch and Oxford are interchangeable postcards with similar buildings, similar names, and similar ancestors.

From Christchurch, I move on to the Southern Alps, which run from top to bottom down the western side of the South Island of New Zealand to form a natural dividing range. There are only three main passes connecting the eastern portion of the South Island with the sparsely populated West Coast. I'm making the journey on the TranzAlpine Express from Christchurch in the east to Greymouth via Arthur's Pass.

New Zealand doesn't have much in the way of passenger trains, the population density is just too small, but the TranzAlpine Express has proven to be a big success with tourists. There are a few locals aboard, but it's like the Glacier Express in Switzerland; mostly sightseers, everyone has a camera cocked and loaded for action.

We're barely underway when a thin, frail man in his sixties hears me talking. His name is Arnold and he stands about 5 feet 2 inches tall and probably weighs no more than 110 pounds on a good day. Arnold grew up on Long Island, the son of a rabbi, eventually making his way to Southern California some 30 years ago. He's now enjoying a splendid retirement with frequent trips abroad.

Arnold recognizes a touch of the American South in my speech and quickly gives me his card. It is inscribed with his name, rank, and the name of his Vermont regiment.

Arnold is a Civil War re-enactor. He lives and breathes the Civil War, for him it's like the war ended last week. He heard my accent and thought I might be someone to talk to. A lot of people think that Southerners still focus on the Civil War, but in reality, we are like most other Americans, many of us can't even tell you the correct century in which the war took place.

We talk about Vicksburg, Gettysburg, Jefferson Davis, and so on . . . or rather, Arnold talks about them. I know enough to slip in an occasional comment but mostly I serve as a listening post, an unwitting, taciturn representative of the Lost Cause. Arnold knows where every unit on both sides fought. He tells me all about his kit, what type of fabric, shoes, and weapons he owns. He knows everything about supplies and material and would have probably made a good quartermaster.

Once we're into the Alps, I break away from Arnold to go to the open-air viewing car and get a better view of the mountains. Arnold follows me; we just passed something that reminded him of the campaign in the Shenandoah Valley, and he's off and running again.

Strangely, I feel good, like I've done a good deed. I've listened patiently, I've helped Arnold enjoy his hobby, I've made his trip a little better.

Now, if I can just get somebody to tell me a little about these mountains we just crossed.

. . .

Nestled between the Tasman Sea and the Southern Alps, the West Coast of the South Island is wild, wet, and rugged. It's not a place for someone looking to lead the soft, easy life. There are large tracts of temperate rainforests and the bush is so green and thick that you can almost watch things grow. It's hard to get to, Kiwis living here are isolated from the rest of the country.

The roaring forties blow unimpeded across the Tasman Sea, dumping large amounts of rain on the sparsely populated area. The West Coast runs 360 miles from north to south but has a population of barely thirty thousand. Much of the native bush has returned and everyone I talked to told me the country is feral. This seems to be the perfect word for describing this area, a tamed area gone wild.

The West Coast was special to the Maori, they would travel to the rivers to harvest greenstone, a form of jade. This was the hardest material available in New Zealand, and the Maori would fashion it into weapons, tools, and ceremonial items. Today it's difficult to find a shop in all of New Zealand that isn't selling greenstone pendants, necklaces, bracelets, etc. Various shapes signify various things to the Maori. I select one design at random to take home, and the Maori salesclerk congratulates me for being a man of peace.

The 2009 IRONMAN® New Zealand incorporated several Maori traditions. At the pasta dinner there were Maori singers and dancers, prior to the swim a waka, or war canoe, patrolled the shore line. Just before the start of the race we witnessed a haka, or war dance. The haka is an aggressive, threatening ritual. Maori men squat and chant forcefully, eyes and tongues protruding, facial tattoos adding to the menacing appearance.

I invariably find the Maori to be genuine people, warm and open, proud of their heritage, anxious to be helpful. They're a big-boned, hearty group, descendants of a people able to paddle thousands of miles across the Pacific. It's an honor to visit their country.

• • •

I feel a little isolated as I drive south from Greymouth, the terminus of the TranzAlpine Express, down the West Coast. It's late summer and everything is dense and dark, the sun never appears. The Tasman Sea on my right crashes on the rocky shore and pushes horizontal sheets of drizzle onto the road. I'm traveling on the main highway, a two lane road that narrows to one lane for bridge crossings. Vehicles going in opposite directions have to take turns in crossing the bridge, but the traffic is so sparse that it isn't much of a problem.

The few people on the road are headed, like me, to see the glaciers. There are at least three thousand of these frozen rivers in the Southern Alps but I'm traveling to see the most visited ones, the Franz Josef Glacier and the Fox Glacier.

This is a unique area; the glaciers descend into a rainforest, ending just a short distance from the Tasman Sea. Some years the glaciers advance a bit, but in general they have been receding. They do flow at a fast rate compared to the glaciers in the Alps of Europe. Watching glaciers flow is a lot like watching trees grow; unless you make repeated visits or take photos, it's a question of faith.

From a short distance away, the Franz Josef looks like a big wall of dirty ice. It seems to need a good scrubbing before being ready for the front of a postcard.

One day I hook up with a guide; we strap on some crampons and go a short way up the glacier. After crossing a few crevasses, we stumble around a little and call it a day. It's a very modest Alpine excursion, commensurate with my experience and abilities.

Later, to get the big picture, I spring for a helicopter ride. We swerve in and out of the mountains, photographing several glaciers that all appear remarkably the same. At one point we stop on the Franz Josef and track around in the snow fields.

All alone atop a glacier, it's a humbling experience. The great disparity between human time and geologic time is astounding.

■ ■ ■

I head from the West Coast eastward through the Southern Alps by way of the Haast Pass. Crossing through vast forests of beech on what used to be an old Maori trail, I continue down through Wanaka and into Queenstown. Along the way I traverse some of the most expensive real estate in the country. This area is often picked as the best place to live in New Zealand.

Queenstown lies on Lake Wakatipu nestled in the shadows of the Remarkables mountain range. The waterfront is packed with adventure outlets, restaurants, coffee bars, outdoor clothing stores, and pubs. The town has a little of the Alpine village ambiance, reminiscent of an anglicized Chamonix or Zermatt. This is the place for the young and rich.

Some of New Zealand's appeal is action and adventure, but most people come simply for the scenic beauty. There's a great variety of landscapes, vegetation, and wildlife; it's a country that bedazzles you at every turn.

New Zealand has fourteen national parks, and the largest and most famous one, Fiordland National Park, takes up the whole southwest corner of the South Island. This park is home to the country's most famous fiord, Milford Sound. No less an authority than Rudyard Kipling called it the Eighth Wonder of the World.

I head from Queenstown to Te Anau, the entry spot into the Milford Sound area. It isn't a big place, mostly motels, restaurants, and outfitters, plus a handful of pubs.

The Moose is my pick for a drinking spot. It is early evening and the pub is virtually empty but I soon hook up with Eddie, a real Kiwi bloke. He appears around sixty or so, a thin, wiry man with leathery skin, a dead ringer for Willie Nelson on Slim-Fast®. Eddie has to have spent his entire working life outdoors. His accent is so thick that it borders on a speech impediment, I have to ask him to repeat every other sentence.

Eddie has been at the bar for a good while, he's at least three drinks ahead of me and anxious to talk. We quickly decide that without cold beer, life would not be worth living. Eddie is a long time helicopter pilot who spends most of his time nowadays shuttling tourists and sportsmen in and out of the Fiordland. He tells me that he has seen and done a lot in his time, but he's convinced that today's world has gone soft and mushy.

I very easily qualify as an old-timer so I have no trouble agreeing. If he thinks it's bad in New Zealand, I tell him, he should come to the United States.

Eddie still flies some deer hunters about but, he tells me, it's not like it was in the old days when his crew would take a hundred or more deer in a single day.

This seems like a big dose of Kiwi bull to me, no one can kill one hundred deer in a day. He can tell that I'm skeptical. Sure they can, he says, you can watch it on YouTube. Eddie fills me in on the details.

New Zealand has no real native mammals, but in the late nineteenth century, red deer were brought from the United Kingdom and released for hunting. New Zealand proved to be the promised land for the deer, it was an ecosystem with no predators, plentiful food, and no hunting allowed.

The deer were in heaven, they thrived and multiplied and soon began eating all the native plants and trees, eventually helping themselves to the grazing land used by livestock.

By the 1930s, the problem was so bad that the hunting of deer was permitted by the government in an effort to control the herd. Unfortunately, many of these areas were so remote and inaccessible that the arrival of hunters did little to thin the deer population.

In the 1970s, when Eddie first got involved, helicopters were introduced. The deer were everywhere and chopper crews, many operating illegally without a license, could kill a hundred or more in a single day.

In those days, Eddie would pilot the helicopter and one or more men would stand in the back shooting the animals. The carcasses were then loaded onto the chopper and flown out for processing.

Guns and helicopters, this is a hell of a story, something that any full-blooded Kiwi would be proud of. I'm duly impressed, but Eddie tells me that there's more.

The 1970s also saw the legalization of deer farming in New Zealand. These animals could be raised like cattle. One thing that all deer farmers need to be successful is live deer for breeding, the more the better. Eddie and his buddies set out to satisfy the demand.

There was no playing around for these boys, this was a man's game. Eddie would locate a deer and fly his chopper just overhead of the fleeing animal. Another buddy in the back would jump from the helicopter onto the back of the running deer, wrestle it to the ground, tie its legs together, and load it into a canvas sack. The chopper would airlift the live animal to a waiting truck for delivery to the farm. At one point, the value of the captured deer for an aspiring farmer reached as high as $1,600.

It's an amazing story, but Eddie makes the whole process sound simple, like picking up a few bags of groceries from the supermarket.

Those were the good old days, Eddie tells me, nothing like the humdrum chores of today. He says the government is making it harder and harder for him to make a living. He and I commiserate about how bad the government rules are. After another beer, we both sound like indentured servants working for an unappreciative government master (that's close to the truth).

Before I leave, I ask Eddie about his remark about YouTube. "Look it up," he tells me. I go back to the hotel and sure enough, there's a clip on

YouTube from the 1970s, dozens of deer being shot from the air. It looks like an airborne abattoir, a brutal sight.

■ ■ ■

The Fiordland, if anything, is undersold. I'm unable to obtain a permit to hike in via the famous Milford Track, it's a one-way journey and the number of hikers is limited. The Milford Track is often described as "the finest walk in the world" but I wouldn't know, I'm forced to sit and ride.

Milford Sound, the largest fiord, is a stunningly beautiful place. Glacier-carved mountains rest in a temperate rainforest, waterfalls tumble down cloud-soaked cliffs, the whole area has a primeval feeling, unchanged in the nearly 250 years since Captain Cook first arrived.

Like so much of New Zealand, you just stand there and gape, mumble a few words to your neighbor, take a couple of photos, and move on to the next thing. Sometimes it seems as if scenic wonders should be handed out in small doses, more time should be allowed for admiration and reflection.

I don't see any of the red deer that my buddy Eddie used to hunt, but I do encounter a few dolphins, lots of seals, and many birds. A guide points out a pair of kea, one of the few alpine parrots.

■ ■ ■

It's a pleasant half-day drive eastward across the South Island from Milford Sound to Dunedin. Like all of the country, the first to live in this area were the Maori, but the main settlement was in the mid-nineteenth century by the Free Church of Scotland. This city is like a small piece of Scotland that had been created and shipped down to New Zealand. Today, Dunedin remains a university town, and for me it's always interesting to meander about and see what today's students are up to. Apparently, the students in New Zealand frequent the same pizza places, fast-food joints, coffee shops, movie rental outlets, and used bookstores as those in the United States. Here the beer comes from pubs but seems to be just as popular as back home.

I'm impressed by a visit to the New Zealand Sports Hall of Fame. The Kiwis have a great athletic tradition, only 4 million people in the country yet they've medaled in every summer Olympic game except two since 1920.

The Hall of Fame is housed on the top floor of the Dunedin Railway Station, an edifice constructed in the Flemish Renaissance style. I can agree with that architectural description, this building would blend right in on the streets of Bruges.

Strangely, I'm the only visitor at the Hall. A man in his seventies awakens from his slumber and hands me a ticket and a pamphlet.

All the great Kiwi distance runners are present: Peter Snell, Rod Dixon, Dick Quax, and John Walker. Edmund Hillary is prominently featured as well as William Hamilton of jet-boat fame. Rugby and yachting are New Zealand favorites, but activities such as shearing and woodchopping are also recognized.

I ask the man at the door why Arthur Lydiard, one of the founders of the modern running movement, is not included. He agrees, Lydiard is a great man and belongs in the Hall of Fame. (Later that day, I read some literature I picked up at the Hall and find out that Lydiard has indeed already been inducted into the Hall of Fame.)

I also mention that in a few years the Hall of Fame will need room for some triathletes (I think you become eligible for entry into the Hall five years after retirement). Hamish Carter and Bevon Docherty have already medaled for the Kiwis in the Olympics, Cameron Brown would seem to be a certain inductee.

After the Hall, I move on to one of New Zealand's little known masterpieces of nature, the Otago Peninsula. This rugged, hilly finger of land extends from the city some twelve miles into the Pacific Ocean.

The peninsula is famous for hosting a breeding colony of Royal Albatrosses. These giant birds have a wingspan of around ten feet and soar gracefully and effortlessly across the skies, dipping down to help themselves to the abundant squid and fish. Unlike many humans, these birds are said to mate for life.

The Otago Peninsula also hosts a big group of Yellow-eyed Penguins. Supposedly, the penguin's closest living relative is the albatross, but after watching the two, I find that hard to believe.

The penguins waddle about upright, dressed in a tuxedo, oblivious to curious humans. Appearing clumsy on land and graceful in the water, the yellow-eyed penguin is one of the rarest species and is found only in New Zealand. They hang out in small groups of a half-dozen or so and avoid the huge colonies seen with many other penguins.

Penguins are a natural draw, lovable, impossible to resist. You find them on logos, in movies, serving as mascots, a staple of children's books and cartoons. Penguins in the land of the Scots, what could be more fun? Breathes there the man with soul so dead, who never to himself hath said, I love penguins.

Natural beauty, wonderful people, delicious food and drink—New Zealand has it all. I hope I get a chance to come back again.

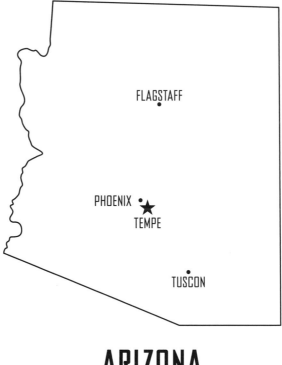

FLAGSTAFF

PHOENIX ★
TEMPE

TUSCON

ARIZONA

Chapter 12
A CROWD IN
THE DESERT
ARIZONA

ONE DAY in my office, a few months after my return from New Zealand, I compare notes with my old friend, Pam. She's a lady who seems to thrive on long distances. Pam has run a marathon in every nook and cranny of the United States, and she just returned from the London Marathon. Pam has a story about every place she has been, she even has time splits for each of her races if you're interested.

I grab this opportunity to tell Pam about my IRONMAN® journeys. Brazil, Switzerland, South Africa, New Zealand—I do my best to make my life sound like a National Geographic special, the near equivalent of climbing Mount Everest blindfolded. Of course, I omit any mention of my mediocre finishing times; there's no point in diminishing my achievements.

Pam's a runner, not a triathlete, and she's like most people when it comes to race times. The numbers are a little foreign, a little vague. Ten hours, twelve hours, fourteen hours, what's the difference? It comes across as a long day any way you look at it.

Pam likes my stories and tells me I should try to finish an IRON-MAN® Triathlon on every continent. According to her, there are a lot of people who try to run a marathon on each continent. She calls this a "noble goal" and makes the whole thing sound like King Arthur and the quest for the Holy Grail.

I've never heard of this "noble goal" before, but I'm not surprised. I once met a man who was crisscrossing the country, running a marathon every week. He said that when his performance began to drop he started reaching for participation points, rather than time. He told me there's even a club for people who run a marathon in all fifty states.

This is the first time the idea has occurred to me; it's the birth of my crazy continental IRONMAN quest. Maybe I can start my own club.

I know there are seven continents but I'm sure I can cross Antarctica off the list. There can't be an IRONMAN Triathlon at the bottom of the world. I saw the pictures of the Antarctic explorers Scott and Shackelton at a bar in Christchurch, New Zealand—those guys could barely walk and they weren't carrying bicycles or swimming gear.

That leaves six continents. Since I didn't do my first IRONMAN Triathlon until age 60, if I can manage all six continents I can lay claim to "Six IRONMAN Triathlons on Six Continents in my Sixties."

The six continent journey is a great idea and I've only got two continents left: North America and Asia.

There are a lot of good races in North America, so I decide to try for number five here in the United States. Florida, Wisconsin, Lake Placid, Coeur d'Alene, they all look good but I pick IRONMAN Arizona. This race is held in November so I'll be able to do my long bike rides and long runs when it's not so blisteringly hot. The older I get, the more the heat bothers me. Plus, the bike and run courses in Arizona don't look very hilly. The older I get, the more the hills bother me. In fact, the older I get, the more *everything* bothers me.

I try to recruit everyone I know to commit to the Arizona project; a big group of friends would make it a fun trip. I get a lot of maybes and half-promises, but in the end, my friends Tony and Steve are the only ones to ante up the wallet-thumping entry fee.

Tony and Steve are a good choice for traveling companions. These guys are definitely better athletes than me, but they're nothing to get too excited about. They'll finish ahead of me, but only by an hour or two. I don't have to worry about being humiliated or embarrassed by racing with any Big Guys.

We play the old game of signing up online a full year in advance, the very moment race registration opens. Even then it's a tenuous thing, the overload seems to crash the system and we can't get through to register. The three of us curse and commiserate, we talk of what might have been. Then later in the day, the computer system gets its second wind and allows us to come onboard.

We're all happy and excited; we're now part of an elite group of people who pay good money to torture themselves. Besides, the race is a year away, for now we can boast and brag; we'll worry about training later on.

■ ■ ■

I'm delighted to be traveling with Tony, he's a great guy. He's a man who owes his very existence and success to IRONMAN® racing.

It's a remarkable story. In his early forties, Tony was floundering about, overweight and underemployed, without a lot going for him. Around this time he got into exercise and managed to eventually finish a marathon or two. Next he was struck by the triathlon bug and just a few short years later he was able to finagle a spot in the IRONMAN World Championship in Kailua-Kona, Hawaii.

Everyone was shocked that he made it to the Big Island, a place normally reserved for the stars of the sport. We were all pleased and surprised when he managed to finish the race before the cutoff time. This is a very prestigious event and we never thought he'd be able to make it.

Word gets around in a small town and the transformation in Tony was astonishing. He appeared on television to talk about his experience, he spoke to local civic clubs and church groups, he even turned up regularly in the local newspaper. Tony strutted about town a new man, confident and secure, sitting atop the athletic world.

There's no end to Tony's IRONMAN world. Today he lives with his young wife and family in a lakeside villa festooned with race memorabilia, it's his own personal museum. He drives a big black pickup truck powered by a V-8 engine and plastered with IRONMAN logos, visible from every angle. You can almost smell the testosterone spewing out of the tailpipe. Most of his conversations include some reference to his Hawaii trip.

Tony even uses his IRONMAN Triathlon as a reference point for the milestones in his life. "I got married two years after my IRONMAN Triathlon," he might say, or, "My daughter was born three years after my trip to Hawaii." The race is an anchor in his life, the linchpin of his very existence.

Steve and I enjoy hearing the details of Tony's adventure. We've heard so much about it over the years that we sometimes feel like we've experienced it ourselves. Some days, it's like that warm Hawaiian breeze blows all the way to Mississippi.

Steve is a solid guy, a salt of the earth, bread and butter, steak-and-potatoes kind of man. In his mid-fifties, he has been delivering mail for over 30 years and has never missed a day of work. If he ran the post office, mail would never get lost or arrive late. In fact, it might even come early.

Steve is just as consistent, just as methodical in his training as in his work; he never takes short cuts. If I can blast myself out of bed in the morning and make it to the local track, I know that Steve will be there doing his duty, pounding out the miles.

Over the years, we've run together so often that we've learned each other's stories. Steve will start a tale about a great race he did in New Orleans a few years back, and I am able to finish the story from memory. He does the same for me including facts about the course, the weather, who else was competing, and so on. He remembers the details I've forgotten and I do the same for him.

Over the years, Steve and I have analyzed and dissected every event we've ever entered. We sometimes forget birthdays and anniversaries but we always remember the time splits from our best races. The minutes and seconds stick in our brains with a permanence that defies the passing years.

Steve and I don't have a lot to boast about but we're both proud to lay claim to a photographic memory, an inerasable record of past athletic performances. We wish it carried over to the rest of our lives, but it doesn't.

■ ■ ■

The swim is held in Tempe Town Lake, a nice two mile long body of water created by damming the Salt River. The lake project was done in the late 1990s, turning a dry river bed into a pleasant spot for boating and fishing. Adjacent parks and pathways were created and upgraded as part of a Rio Salado Master Plan. Close to Arizona State University, the whole complex is made to order for hosting an IRONMAN® Triathlon.

Tempe Town Lake has a lot to offer, but I'll always remember it as the site of my head-on swimming collision. Through a combination of clumsiness, stupidity, and ignorance, I was able to turn a simple practice swim into a near concussion and a major facial laceration.

What a bizarre accident. Normally, as long as you avoid drowning, swimming is one of the safest sports around. It's easy on the muscles and joints. An IRONMAN® Triathlon is full of problems waiting to happen, but I managed to find trouble where none is supposed to exist. I have to be one of the few people to ever need suturing after swimming, maybe I should start wearing a helmet or carrying my own airbag when I get in the water.

For two or three days before the race, officials set aside a few hours each morning for a practice swim. It's a good time to check out the water temperature, get some course bearings, and make sure that there are no problems with your wetsuit or goggles. I normally drastically decrease my training for a couple of weeks before an IRONMAN Triathlon and at times I think that I may have forgotten how to swim. The ritual of a short swim gives me a little reassurance.

At the practice swim, hundreds of swimmers mill about, coming and going at various times. Some are like me, just doing an easy ten minute swim, while others seem to be sprinting to stardom. Everyone climbs down the metal stairway, jumps into the lake, and turns immediately toward the starting line. The start is about a hundred yards from the steps leading into the water.

I plunge in and stop to catch my breath. This water is cold, my face is numb and I start to get a headache. I begin swimming and go less than a quarter mile when suddenly I feel like I've been struck on the forehead with a ball hammer. I'm stunned, disoriented, and a little dizzy. After a few seconds, I realize that I've had a head-on collision with another swimmer coming from the opposite direction.

The two of us mumble apologies and head on our way. A nearby swimmer asks me if I'm okay and tells me that I'm bleeding. I can see and feel the warm stream of blood running down my face, coating my goggles. I've picked up a large cut extending a couple of inches along my brow line and I'm bleeding like a stuck pig. I received a head butt laceration. It doesn't seem fair, I'm just getting in a practice swim and I've managed to split my head open.

I'm really angry with the man who cracked me in the head, I'm ready to call him to account (should I suggest Round Two?). Then Tony points to a sign at the entrance to the swim that says something like "keep to the right."

I was going the wrong way, a man in the wrong place at the wrong time. It was my fault, I've only got myself to blame.

As I climb out of the water, bright red blood continues to pour down my face. This is crazy, I feel foolish and embarrassed. Everyone offers assistance; a couple of towels do nothing to stem the flow. A crowd gathers around to see if this elderly gentleman will be carted off on a stretcher. Finally an EMT offers some gauze pads and tape. There's a hospital a mile or so down the road, he tells me, I need to go and be checked.

Tony and Steve are very concerned and finally begin to treat me with the respect and consideration I've deserved all along. We stop at a local drugstore and get some fancy Band-Aids®. I buy several types and sizes, hoping that at least one will work. Back at the motel room I shower and wash away all the dried blood. The bandages have stopped the bleeding, but I know if the laceration reopens during the race it could be a problem. So, I head to the local emergency room and proudly present my Medicare card. My card is just two weeks old. The bright red white and blue colors haven't even had time to fade.

The lady at the ER smiles, returns my card and asks me to have a seat. I spend the next two hours in the waiting room catching up on old issues of *Ladies Home Journal*, while Steve and Tony head out to drink beer and eat lunch.

They arrive back at the hospital about the same time I'm finally carried back to a cubicle in a back room. They've discovered a good Irish pub down the road and they swear they will check back with me a little later.

There are five or six cubicles in my new home in the bowels of the hospital and they're all empty. This place is eerie; no one comes in, not a nurse, technician, or doctor. I wait for another two hours in complete silence. I've practiced medicine for 40 years, and I've never been in an ER like this. I wonder if they placed me in the morgue by mistake.

This is the one day allotted for picking up your registration packet. I have to personally retrieve it by 5:00 p.m., or else I will have to walk back to Mississippi (race officials don't say it quite this strongly, but it's almost as serious).

I have little choice, so I get up, walk out through the same door I came in, and head to race registration. No one says anything, no one notices, no one cares. Are they alive in this ER? Is this a mausoleum disguised as a hospital?

I decide to leave my fancy Band-Aid undisturbed. I pack a lot of extra bandages in my transition and special needs bags. If necessary, I'll patch myself up as needed along the way.

I tell Steve and Tony my new plans but they don't seem interested. They are arguing over which is the best beer—Guinness® or Harp. They're laughing and giggling like teenagers out on the town.

I need to keep a better eye on these boys.

■ ■ ■

Race morning is cool and crisp with a perfect sunrise. Here in the desert things have a sharp-edged clarity, as if finely chiseled and scrubbed raw by the autumn sun. I wait until the last moment to plunge into the frigid Town Lake. After my collision during the practice swim, I'm a little gun shy. Another bump could reopen my tender forehead laceration. I jump in, swim a hundred yards to the starting line, and begin to tread water, awaiting the gun.

Treading water in a wetsuit is easy, you just stand there. You can't sink, the wetsuit is a personal flotation device, no movement is required.

This is reassuring, there's no way I can sink and drown before the start, that's one less thing I have to worry about.

The starting cannon sounds, and after a couple of hundred yards, the chill is gone. Not only that, the thrill is gone. There are 2,500 swimmers fighting for the same spot and there's enough thrashing and bumping to warm any body of water. It's what someone once called hand-to-foot combat.

The course is straight down and straight back with a bridge at the beginning and at the turnaround. These bridges are simple landmarks to strive for, you see them from the very start. Every time you look up, the span appears tantalizingly close, but after a while it seems to recede rather than come nearer.

The pushing and shoving goes on for the entire 2.4 miles but I finally climb out of the water at 1:32.

There are dozens of wetsuit strippers waiting to lend a helping hand. The early sun feels warm and refreshing, and I'm soon off on the three loop bike course.

With this many competitors and three loops, things are crowded the entire way. I am constantly passing and being overtaken, there's a continuous in-and-out and back-and-forth flow of bikers.

If you ever want to draft without trying to draft, IRONMAN® Arizona is the place to be. It's impossible not to get tugged along for a few seconds as bikers come by in quick succession. I make a halfhearted, insincere effort to stay out of the slipstream.

The bike course very quickly leaves the city of Tempe and heads into the Salt River Pima-Maricopa Indian Community (SRPMIC). After a few miles and a handful of turns you're past Sun Devil stadium, through the seemingly endless rows of muffler shops, pizza restaurants, and strip malls, and into the desert.

It's a pleasant day and I'm feasting on a trove of chocolate chip cookies I've brought along. For me, when it comes to fluids, too much is better than too little, and as a result I'm having to make regular pit stops. Race officials have warned everyone to use the porta-toilet rather than relieving themselves *au naturel*. The problem is that there are only a few toilets at each aid station, and there are lines of athletes waiting to use them. I didn't come to Arizona to wait in line to take a leak, I came to race.

So, I use a clever ruse, a tactic so devious that no one else appears to have thought of it. Whenever the urge strikes me, I pull over to the side of the road (there are no trees in the desert), get off my bike, bend over and act like I'm working on my bike and go about my business. No waiting in line for me.

It never ceases to amaze me, in an IRONMAN® Triathlon your concerns are whittled down to such a primitive basic level—moving your arms and legs, breathing, drinking, eating, urinating, staying cool. Life is stripped bare, reduced to the essentials. It's a very simple calculation. If you can keep everything going for a thousand minutes or so, you'll make it to the finish line.

That's enough time for the philosophical contemplation of bodily functions. I'm looking for Tony and Steve on the bike. I know that Tony started before me, hopefully Steve finished the swim and will soon be catching me. It's always hard for me to pick out someone on the bike. Everyone wears a goofy-looking helmet and all bikes look remarkably similar. The colors are different but the shapes are the same, sometimes I can't even tell if it's a man or a woman coming from the opposite direction. Maybe it's because they are going so fast or maybe it's because my vision is on par with my heart and lungs.

Around mile 100 Steve passes me on the bike and I discreetly grab onto his wheel for a mile or two. He glances back and yells, "Have you no shame?" humiliating me in front of some other cyclists, so I drop back. That's the last time I'll listen to his stories. Still, I'm into the second transition area a little ahead of schedule.

The marathon course consists of three loops around Town Lake and adjacent parks. For me this is the most current episode of what I call the Journey to Hell. It's the same as every previous race: intermittent running and walking, hour after hour of constant pain and suffering, hurting in a dozen different ways. The paths and roads are mostly concrete and my joints feel like someone removed the shock absorbers. I seem to get a big jolt with each step. This has got to be the advance guard of approaching arthritis.

Yet for an IRONMAN® Triathlon, it's not a bad day and I finish in 14:48, a Ponce de Leon performance in my book. The best I've done since Brazil.

Tony and Steve managed 13:15 and 13:27 and we are all glad to survive the ordeal. It's a happy day when everyone struggles home.

■ ■ ■

The day after the race, Steve, Tony, and I head over to the race headquarters to pick up some gear we left behind. We encounter two long lines extending several blocks along the walkway. There are some tired looking bodies warming in the morning sun.

One line is for those hardy souls waiting to register in person for next year's race. By showing up onsite, these people will beat the online registration crunch that starts the following day. It's the best way to secure a spot in the race. As we learned ourselves, computer registration can wreak havoc with the best-laid plans.

The pent-up demand for IRONMAN races never ceases to amaze me. Many of these folks have driven long distances to stand in line to register for next year's event. In good times and in bad times, the demand for IRONMAN continues to grow. Will there ever be enough IRONMAN Triathlons to satisfy the needs and desires of all the aspiring masochists in the world? How high will the entry fee go? Is $1,000 just around the corner?

We all laugh at those people waiting patiently in line, ready to shell out hard-earned dollars to pursue their quixotic quest. It's a fool's errand and we'll have none of it. We are all finishers.

After chuckling at those strange people with misplaced priorities, we fall in like sheep in the other line. This is the line for those folks waiting to enter the IRONMAN® store.

You can't simply walk in and spend half a month's rent on overpriced IRONMAN merchandise, you must first wait quietly, standing on legs that feel like concrete pillars. Then, a few at a time, you are allowed to enter the Promised Land, wander about, and give your credit card a true IRONMAN workout.

The overseas races don't have this kind of demand. IRONMAN kitsch has reached its highest level in the United States. It's IRONMAN idolatry in its purest form.

I'm ready to do my part to support the IRONMAN economy. I've got a closet full of gear but I damn sure don't have enough. How many ways can you print the IRONMAN name and logo on a tee shirt? A lot more than you might think; a creative person could wear a different outfit every week of the year.

I manage to grab the last bike jersey for Steve in his size. A few water bottles, a sticker, and a wonderful $15 coffee mug complete my purchase.

All three of us are happy, content, and a few dollars poorer. The cash registers at the store are so overworked and hot that they're about to explode.

We all agree, we must come back to shop later in the day to make sure we didn't overlook anything.

■ ■ ■

Steve has to head home right after the race, but Tony and I have a couple of days to look around the Tempe area. I decide to visit the Desert Botanical Garden, just a couple of miles from our hotel. It's an easy walk, a chance to loosen up the legs.

The Desert Botanical Garden is a wonderful place to learn about desert flora and fauna. There are over twenty-thousand plants covering some fifty acres or so. This is a different world, unlike anything I've ever seen.

The Garden has several trails and exhibits that highlight different ecosystems. I particularly like the one that shows how Native Americans survived using the available plants for food, shelter, tools, and basket making.

Quite honestly, these desert dwellers deserve a tip of the hat. The Sonoran Desert doesn't look like much at first glance, it's not the kind of place you would want to go on your honeymoon, yet there's a lot more to it than meets the eye. The Native Americans put everything to good use and have perfected the art of making a lot out of a little.

The following day I am able to drag Tony along to visit the Heard Museum, an extraordinary collection of Southwest Native American art. There are seemingly endless galleries of baskets, pottery, jewelry, clothing, and other objects. Barry Goldwater's collection of Hopi Kachina dolls is prominently featured.

There's also a moving exhibit dealing with Indian boarding schools and the "Americanization" of Native Americans.

For me, the Heard Museum is time well spent, but for Tony, I'm not so sure. He has got bigger things on his mind. He spends most of the day trying to figure out how to best display his new IRONMAN® memorabilia, plus he's polishing his new race stories. Tony's star is rising so fast that he has trouble hanging on to it. As for me, I need to get to work. Asia is the final stop on my six-continent journey.

BEIJING •

XI'AN •

SHANGHAI •

HAIKOU
HAINAN

CHINA

Chapter 13
THE SIXTH AND FINAL STOP
CHINA

WHEN I was a young child, my playmates and I would sometimes dig with our shovels in the backyard of my grandfather's home. It was a large lot with a couple of fruit trees, some trash cans, and a lot of open space, nothing that would ever qualify for *Better Homes and Gardens*, but we loved it. Pop never seemed to mind us poking about, he even encouraged us. He said that if we dug deep enough, we would eventually reach China.

At age seven or eight that seemed like a feasible project. We figured that if we all chipped in and took turns, we should reach the Orient in just a few days. We were eager and ambitious, but we also had a good underlying reason to work away.

In the 1950s, China was full of poor starving children who would have been delighted to eat any food that we left on our plates. At least that's what all the adults at home and at school told us. We envisioned China as a handy place to dispose of things like liver, broccoli, and cauliflower. In our minds, these dishes didn't belong on our plates, they belonged in the local landfill.

Our group worked for several days but never got much deeper than a couple of feet in the ground. We soon lost interest, but we always regarded China as a mysterious and forbidden place.

Today, things are different, but China still qualifies in my mind as a remote and exotic land, a place where the very old and the very new constantly clash. A country that focuses on its past in order to justify the present.

Haikou is several stops from my home in Hattiesburg, Mississippi, but my bike and I survive. My body is compressed, congealed, dehydrated, and shrunk. This is pure ergonomic misery.

The days before the race are the usual mixture of unpacking and assembling my bicycle, attending race briefings, taking a tour of the bike and run courses, and squeezing in a practice swim.

Any IRONMAN® Triathlon is a major event. There are barely thirty or so in the entire world, and they all require large amounts of money, hundreds of volunteers, and countless hours of work to stage. It's not something that your local civic club puts together on the spur of the moment.

IRONMAN China is no exception, it's one of very few IRONMAN Triathlons held in Asia. It's also a wonderful opportunity for China, the top gold medal winner at the 2008 Olympics, to show off its athletic prowess, to once again impress the world.

There's just one problem: no one seems to have invited the Chinese, or maybe the IRONMAN race just isn't on their map.

China is inching toward a population of 1.5 billion, and many economists think that there are three hundred million people in the country with a lifestyle close to that of the United States. It's a vast and varied nation with many prosperous consumers. Yet, very few of these people seem to have taken up the sport of triathlon. The 2010 IRONMAN® China has just a couple of dozen entrants from China.

Why is this race such an endangered species in China? I'm sure there are many reasons. The Chinese are typically viewed as a shrewd and practical people who very much value balance and harmony. It's not a nation given to silly excesses. If ever there was an event designed to derange, disturb, and destroy the normal rhythm of life, it's the IRON-MAN Triathlon. There's no yin or yang in this race, just pain and suffering. Most Chinese find it hard to imagine that anyone of sound mind would do an IRONMAN Triathlon.

Maybe this is what 5,000 years of civilization does for a country, or maybe the Chinese are just a little smarter than the rest of us.

Comparatively speaking, the 2010 IRONMAN China is much less crowded than other races. Most races reach two thousand entrants, but only four hundred are registered for this race. There's also an IRON-MAN® 70.3® race being staged the same day, and a few more Chinese are entered in this event. Still, there are many more foreigners than Chinese.

Overall there is a large group of Japanese and Australian competitors; these countries having strong triathlon communities. Many of the other competitors are Westerners living and working in Asia, every major U.S. company seems to be trying to do business in China. Plus there are a lot of people in the race like me, people who like to travel and use this as an excuse to hit the road.

China is a long way from home and this race proves to be one too far for me. Travel broadens the mind, but it can also wreak havoc with the digestive tract. A bout of food poisoning with vomiting and diarrhea, plus intrepid jet lag set me up for the final blows of heat, humidity, and wind. In hindsight, I knew I was in for a bigger challenge than I anticipated.

∎ ∎ ∎

On race day morning, there's none of the usual pre-dawn stillness. It's dark, overcast, and very windy. The tents and flags in the transition area are whipping about madly. If you need to talk to your neighbor, you have to shout. It's already 79 degrees and it's not even daylight (I check my temperature gauge on my bicycle like a diabetic checks his glucose meter, hoping for good news). There are a lot of young Chinese girls in race tee-shirts wandering about, repeatedly saying, "Good morning." I ask one where I can get some water, she replies, "Good morning."

The swim course is an unusual four loop route in the Nandu River, supposedly designed to minimize the current. In reality, one-half of the course is with the current and the other is against. A strong current on the swim is like a strong wind on the bike. The struggle into the wind or current is always difficult; the return journey is only slightly less of a problem.

When I signed up for this race it was advertised as a point-to-point swim course with the current at your back, designed to produce "record swim times." Everyone was assured in advance of a personal best in the swim leg. There was even a nice little map showing you entering the river upstream, swimming the entire way with the current, and exiting downstream. It looked more like a float trip down the Nandu than a long-distance swim.

Unfortunately, this was not to be. On race day, there is no point-to-point course, no record time. Like much of the 2010 IRONMAN® China, things are vague, uncertain, and subject to change. At the race briefing a lot of questions go unanswered, uncertainty hovers about. There's a permanent undercurrent of insecurity, nothing feels quite right.

There are four loops and the young swimmers start early, while the old age groups go last. As a result, I spend my second and third laps being beaten and pummeled, treated like a floating punching bag. The Big

Guys see no reason to swim around me, they simply go right over me, pushing my frail body to the bottom of the mighty Nandu.

Despite battling the currents and my fellow competitors, I'm out of the water in a decent time, 1:37. I spend a good ten minutes trying to get out of my wetsuit while the group of young Chinese girls watch and giggle. Some say, "Good job," while for others it's still "Good morning."

Out on the bike, my temperature gauge reads ninety degrees and the headwind is horrible, it's a boisterous breeze. What little energy I have is quickly sucked dry by the blowing inferno.

Once we exit the city, the roads are new and modern with no traffic. Most of the route is on a sterile highway with just open fields, heat, and wind; it's a visit to the devil's furnace. Around thirty miles, the course exits the highway and climbs up and through a couple of old villages. The peasants are in the rice fields working while water buffalo wander about, dumping their calling cards in large piles. Avoiding buffalo dung becomes an important priority. Groups of Chinese cluster in the villages, the children cheer while the adults stare.

This is a great experience; it's like dropping back a century or two in time. Like all of China, the city and the countryside are different worlds. Still, the whole thing makes me a little uneasy. I'm riding a bicycle that costs more than many of these people make in five years, and it doesn't seem appropriate or just. I've been to *favelas* in Brazil and townships in South Africa, and I had the same feeling in all those places. I try to learn from, and appreciate, less economically developed cultures; they take nothing for granted and do a lot with a little.

Heading back into the city there's not much of a tailwind; the wind is now coming from the side. The wind has been so strong; I've had to stay out of my aerobars for fear of being blown out of control. My gauge says 99 degrees and I'm well done, more than fully cooked. At every aid station, I stop and drink copiously and douse myself with water. The fluids are nauseatingly warm, like drinking from a hot tub. The Chinese are clever—they invented gunpowder, printing, and the compass, among other things— but they've never gotten the hang of making ice.

The bike course is two loops and at the end of the first loop I stop. It's an almost unconscious decision. There's no negotiating, my body decides it's time to quit, regardless of what my mind might think. I saw it all coming days ago.

If my IRONMAN® saga was a Greek tragedy, this would be a good spot for the chorus to appear and bemoan the fall of the hero. Fortunately, there's no chorus, no fanfare, no gnashing of the teeth. It's a very ordinary end of the affair, not the spiritual death penalty I thought it would be.

I climb off my bike and take it to the transition area. A few other athletes have just bailed out, the race director tells me three times to make sure I turn in my timing chip (race officials don't really mind if you die in a triathlon as long as you first turn in your chip).

I'm stuck at midday under the blistering Chinese sun, searching for shade, wishing for a cool drink. The wind continues to blow mightily and the sun bears down. A young Chinese girl tells me, "Good morning." It's a quiet, disappointing ending.

It's been a tough day, about a third of the competitors failed to finish, but that of course means that two-thirds made it home. Those warnings you hear on television every summer during a heat wave are true; high temperatures are particularly dangerous for the elderly. Only one of the eight entrants in my age group managed to finish. I'm disappointed for myself but I take no pleasure in other's misfortunes, that's a loser's game. Plus, I'm not about to wrap myself in a blanket of shame and despair.

The wonderful, mysterious, complex country of China awaits and I'm ready to go hit the road. Good morning, China.

■ ■ ■

I'm a true babe-in-the-woods when it comes to getting around in China. I can't speak or read Chinese and the vast majority of Chinese can't speak or read English. I do better deciphering hieroglyphics than I do reading a street sign or a menu in China. The barrier is near total; it's like trying to communicate with the birds in the sky.

Despite this giant language gap, I get along fine. I've managed to learn a few basic words and phrases in Chinese, and I toss them out to everyone I meet, sort of like I'm handing out dollar bills. *Ni hao*, I say (hello) on first encounter, then *mei wenti* (no problem) when they stare at me, plus *xie xie* (thank you).

Invariably I get an unintelligible response that probably translates along the line of "you foreign dumbass, if you knew how stupid you sounded, you'd probably keep your mouth shut." This doesn't bother me at all, for all I know they might well be saying, "Welcome honored guest, we are blessed and enriched by your visit."

The Chinese have a special word for people like me. I'm a *laowai*, a foreigner. I come from a less evolved, less sophisticated civilization, one that falls far short of China's five thousand glorious years. I'm an intruder, a barbarian, a fool, or at best a curiosity. I've played the useful idiot role before, so I offer up a goofy smile and a half bow and invariably receive the same in return.

In France, Spain, Germany or even Russia, you can look at signs and make an honest guess at their meaning. These languages have a lot in common; they're simply variations of a common tongue.

Not the case in China. Instead of letters like much of the world, the Chinese use characters. There are somewhere around twenty thousand of these little fellows, but you only need to know three thousand or so to read a newspaper. Some characters represent pictures or ideas but most have a phonetic component. They're a combination of meaning and sound.

The Chinese are helpful, though. They've translated the characters into letters that we *laowai* are familiar with, a system called *pinyin*. Scholars say they've romanized the language. In any case, the letters are easier than the random lines of the Chinese characters, and they allow me to take a stab at Chinese words.

The Chinese have thrown in another obstacle to keep an old-timer *laowai* like me from learning Chinese. They've created a tonal bag of tricks. There are four basic tones. If you say a word or phrase in one tone, it means one thing (I'll skip the dog meat, thanks). If you say the very same words in another tone, it means something entirely different (if you will, supersize that order of ox penis).

China can be full of fun and surprises.

■ ■ ■

A couple of days after the race I join a group of *laowai* for a trip around China. It's a small crowd of 15 people from the United States, Canada, and Australia, mostly athletes who competed in the 2010 IRONMAN® China, plus friends and family members.

These are some of the most interesting and most accomplished people that I've ever traveled with. We all share a similar interest and as a result there's an ease and comfortableness that comes from not having to explain why you travel to the four corners of the Earth and pay good money to push your body and soul to the point of collapse.

Our guide Michael looks about 40 years old and comes from the southern part of Hainan Island. Michael, like most Chinese who have studied English, adopted an English name early in his studies. These English nicknames are an interesting phenomenon. I've run across a few strange names (Apple, Dragon, Fort, etc.) but many seem to have been taken from a Jane Austen novel (Reginald, Joshua, Lucy, Marianne, etc.) There seem to be very few modern names.

Michael's language skills are home grown, but he and I hit it off well. I enjoy his brief and pithy insights, delivered in a fortune cookie style. He has a great sense of humor and a genuine pride of his country.

The first stop on our tour is the ancient city of Xi'an. Once the capital of China, it was the eastern terminus of the Silk Road, a network of trade routes that connected Asia to the Mediterranean world.

During the Dark Ages, when Europe was muddling along and the Renaissance was centuries away, Chinese civilization was in full bloom. In the seventh and eighth centuries when London, Paris, and Rome were small settlements, Xi'an was the largest city in the world with a population of more than a million people.

This period is the famous Tang Dynasty, a high point in Chinese civilization. It's a landmark for today's China, a source of pride, a reminder of the country's ancient, great, and glorious history.

In the old days, the Silk Road used to draw the merchants to Xi'an, but today the streets are filled with tourists. The city is a regular stop on the standard foreigner's tour of China.

The first thing that strikes you on arrival isn't the splendor of ancient China but rather the horrible air pollution. The air is thick and heavy, a yellow-gray color, your eyes and nose feel the sting, visibility is limited, the horizon fades quickly into an ugly fog.

The major source of pollution is coal. China is a huge coal burning nation. All the other usual suspects also contribute to the problem: increasing construction, growing automobile traffic, more heavy industry, desertification with growing sandstorms. The Kyoto Protocol has yet to touch home in China.

In Xi'an, we visit the Big Wild Goose Pagoda, a Buddhist temple dating from the seventh century. It's about seven stories tall but I decide to make the long climb to the top for a sweeping view of the city. It's midday but the entire city is cast in a fog, like the opening scene of a crime movie. I expect to see Humphrey Bogart emerge from the shadows, but instead I get a glimpse of a tour group from South Carolina (they all are sporting Gamecock logos), but not much else. They're milling about, searching for their tour bus, fiddling with their cameras, noisy and excited like schoolchildren.

In the past 20 years, China has rebuilt many Buddhist and Taoist temples destroyed during the Cultural Revolution. The People's Republic is officially an atheist country, religion went out when the communists came in. According to the government, China guarantees freedom of religion and recognizes five religions—Buddhism, Taoism, Islam, Catholicism, and Protestantism.

Xi'an has a massive city wall surrounding the downtown area. It dates from the Ming dynasty and the fourteenth century and runs some eight miles around the oldest part of the city. On the average, the wall is forty feet high and forty feet wide. It's a nice place to stretch the legs. You can rent a bike or take a pleasant walk. Some even come in November when Xi'an stages a marathon atop the Ming wall; strong lungs are a necessity.

One evening we attend a dinner show featuring the music and dance of the Tang dynasty. Chinese officials are rightfully proud of this period in the country's history and they spare no expense in putting the country's best foot forward. Everything is excellent: the food, music, costumes, dance. I love these cultural shows. Sometimes they're flabby performances, designed more to separate the tourist from his hard-earned dollar than to entertain and enlighten, but some of my fondest travel memories have come from tourist-based cultural events. This is the best I've ever seen anywhere.

The Terracotta Warriors are also a sight to behold. They have earned a spot as one of China's big three tourist attractions, along with the Great Wall and the Forbidden City. The Chinese have dubbed them the Eighth Wonder of the World.

The army is a collection of over eight thousand terra cotta sculptures made during the time of the first emperor of China, Qin Shi Huang. These sculptures date from around 210 B.C., but were only discovered in 1974 by some local farmers digging a well a few miles outside of Xi'an.

Before viewing the army, we get an opportunity, at a convenient souvenir factory, to see how the figures were constructed. Large workshops produced the head, arms, legs, and torso separately. Since the emperor had decreed that no two figures were to be alike, a lot of time was spent fashioning different facial features. All the parts were then joined in assembly line fashion, and the units were fired. A color lacquer finish was added, and real weapons and armor completed the project. The final warriors vary in size, but most are around six feet high.

The actual soldiers are displayed in three large pits. While the site contains an estimated eight thousand figures, less than two thousand have been excavated. Many were destroyed a few years after the first emperor's death by some unhappy warlords. All of the pits contain numerous fragments as well as the complete figures. As a result, careful reconstruction is a long-term, ongoing process, a never ending jigsaw puzzle.

This is a very popular site. There are tourists from all over the world strolling along the elevated walkways, looking down on the pits containing the figures. The soldiers stand in long columns just as they were found, in formation, ready to go to battle in the afterworld.

■ ■ ■

Everyone tells you that today's China is a mixture of the ancient and the modern, a place where the old gives way grudgingly to the new. Nowhere is this dichotomy more striking than in Shanghai, a city where the spur and lash of commerce do battle with the old traditions.

The modern jumps out immediately upon arrival in Shanghai. There's a brand-new airport staffed by well-dressed young men and women, a recently completed magnetic levitation train that travels around twenty miles to the city center reaching a speed of 269 miles per hour, and enough new skyscrapers dotting the skyline to make Manhattan seem like a provincial backwater.

One of our first stops in the Shanghai wonderland is the Oriental Pearl Tower. Completed in 1994, this spaceship-looking building seems like a relic of the old days, it's almost a fossil by Shanghai skyscraper standards. Nevertheless, it has everything a modern-day tourist could desire—a revolving restaurant, a shopping mall, an observation deck, and thousands of screaming Chinese children in constant motion. It's not unlike visiting Seattle or San Antonio.

The view from the Oriental Pearl Tower is stunning. The Shanghai area is awash in new buildings, it's a true forest of skyscrapers. The most majestic of all is the Shanghai World Financial Center. It's the tallest building in China and it houses the world's highest hotel. Shaped like a giant bottle opener, the World Financial Center is the most distinctive of all the Shanghai giants.

Running alongside the Huangpu River is Shanghai's most famous area, the Bund. There you'll find all the art deco and neoclassical style buildings that once housed the grand hotels, banks, and trading houses that were symbols of western commercial dominance.

• • •

Sometimes your own ignorance can bowl you over. Your lack of knowledge about a subject is so absolute, so complete that you wonder where you've been for the last six decades. How could you not know anything about something so important?

And so it is with the traditional Chinese garden.

I grew up in the rural South where the garden was a place to grown butter beans, okra, and squash or, on a higher plane, a lovely setting for azaleas, camellias, and dogwoods.

The Chinese garden transcends simple horticulture, it's a work of art, something every bit important to the Chinese as literature, calligraphy, and music. The Chinese garden is elaborate, complex, and a bit mysterious; there's a meaning for everything, nothing is random. Symbolism and balance are the order of the day. It's above all a place for meditation and enlightenment, a spot for the contemplation of nature.

It's not a question of planting some trees and bushes with a few flower beds thrown in for good measure. A Chinese garden is a meticulously constructed area of rocks, water, plants, and buildings arranged in a specific order. Limestone rocks from certain lakes are highly treasured, water gives balance and acts as a mirror of the surroundings as well as a home for goldfish, a symbol of good fortune. Bamboo represents strength, pine trees longevity, peonies wealth, and so on. Pavilions and halls are carefully placed in order to produce spots for viewing idealized scenes.

In the Chinese garden, everything is in balance, the yin and the yang are alive and well and doing whatever they're supposed to do. I tell Michael that I honestly believe that I'm too ignorant to become properly enlightened. I come from the school of thought where a tree represents a tree, where rocks are rocks, and bodies of water are places for fish to live.

"John," he replies, "you come live in China, I make you smart man." He's not smiling, this *laowai* needs help. I'm again reminded that I'm a heathen and a savage afoot in China.

I may be ignorant, but I'm an open-minded man, ready to adopt the oriental mindset. I take a long stroll around Yuyuan Garden in the old central part of Shanghai. This garden features a beautiful temple and a lovely teahouse, but there's no peace and tranquility.

There are thousands of Chinese packed along the pathways and they're not searching for enlightenment, they're looking for a good spot to take a photograph. I'm pushed along in a sea of Chinese and do my best to avoid a swarm of cigarette smokers before exiting the garden to meander around the adjacent bazaar. The stalls are packed with ancient Chinese crafts, ancient Chinese medicines, and not so ancient Chinese souvenirs. It's a forced march through a perilous gauntlet of consumerism. Chairman Mao items compete for shelf space with Elvis Presley mementos.

Yuyuan Garden is nice but if you're really interested in Chinese gardens (and Michael our guide tells us that we are indeed very interested) then the place to go is the nearby city of Suzhou.

Suzhou is the center of China's silk industry and is famous for its gardens and stone bridges. We visit several gardens including the Humble Administrator's Garden, considered by many to be the finest garden in all of China.

In the sixteenth century, the Humble Administrator retired and constructed his garden. He was no ordinary bureaucrat; in those days imperial officials were scholars and poets, the kind of men capable of constructing a metaphysical masterpiece in no time at all.

Today, the garden is a series of pavilions, halls, bridges, and lakes, separate yet connected in a mazelike fashion. Each turn produces a new portrait, a lovely tableau worthy of any artist. The Chinese garden is a long way from the butter bean fields of Mississippi. I think I've got a lot to learn.

• • •

The next day, our group is delayed on our flight into Beijing. The previous day the city had experienced a massive sandstorm with visibility so reduced that the airport had to be closed. On arrival, the air is still thick and yellow, there's a film of sand coating everything in town; it looks like a scene from *Lawrence of Arabia*.

The sands of time are on the move in China but no one in Beijing appears to have noticed. This is another one of those Chinese ecological disasters brewing under the surface. Close to thirty percent of the country is now desert, and each year desertification claims another nine hundred miles or so. The Gobi Desert is marching toward Beijing and currently is less than one hundred and fifty miles away.

Still, for Beijing residents it appears to be business as usual, there are maybe a few more people wearing face masks, but no one is staying inside. The Chinese deal with life as it is.

Tiananmen Square is at the heart of modern Beijing and is ground zero for the worship of Mao Zedong. An enormous portrait of Chairman Mao, the Great Helmsman, rests over the Gate of Heavenly Peace, staring serenely over Tiananmen Square.

Mao is China and China is Mao and you're never allowed to forget it. Everywhere you go you see his face. The Chairman's picture is on not one denomination, but every single piece of paper currency. No matter what you buy, you pay with Mao. The memorabilia is unending: coins, stamps, pens, pencils, key chains, cigarette lighters, wrist watches, CDs, cups and saucers, tee-shirts. You thought IRONMAN® memorabilia was a big business, wait until you meet Chairman Mao.

Tiananmen Square is massive, said to be able to hold a million people. There's no vehicular traffic so it's a good place to stroll about and breathe in the thick, brown air.

The giant portrait of Chairman Mao at one end looks past the Monument to the People's Heroes to his very own mausoleum. Thousands gather early in the day to stand and wait for hours for a chance to view the personal remains of their man. Mao's waxen body is raised from its refrigerated home each day just in time for the throngs of worshippers.

You'd think it would be something like visiting the Lincoln Memorial but this is serious business for the Chinese. Mao inspires the same rapture and devotion that I've seen at the various shrines to the Virgin Mary across the Catholic world. School groups, tour groups, older men and women, they all seem greatly moved by the Great Helmsman's embalmed corpse.

We pass under the portrait of Chairman Mao to gain entry into the Forbidden City. The Chinese call this seventy-eight acre complex the Palace Museum. It was once home to the emperors of the last two dynasties, the Ming and the Qing. At one time, it was the very center of the Chinese universe, the exclusive domain of the emperor and his court, an area seen by very few people.

It may have once been a forbidden place, but the Chinese are making up for the centuries of exclusion as half the nation seems to be visiting the Forbidden City at the same time. As we pass through the Meridian Gate, enormous crowds of tourists propel us through the three giant halls—the Hall of Supreme Harmony, the Hall of Middle Harmony, and the Hall of Preserving Harmony. The layout has a three little pigs logic to it. It's the usual crush for photographs, every Chinese wants his picture taken next to a dragon.

Eventually, we pass through the Gate of Heavenly Purity into the Inner Court, a complex that includes the palaces and living quarters of the emperor.

The visit to the Forbidden City is a one-way journey that takes two or three hours. I am very impressed by the Forbidden City, it's a magnificent architectural complex. If I could visit just one sight in all of China this would probably be the one. On the other hand, I might choose the Great Wall of China.

The Wall is actually a series of fortifications stretching about four thousand miles across northern China. Some portions are simple earthen mounds while others are massive stone walls. They've been built and rebuilt over the centuries dating at least back to the Emperor Qin Shi Huang (our friend of Terracotta Warrior fame).

The Wall snakes and undulates, following the contours of the colorless mountains. It stretches over the rocky peaks for as far as the eye can see, dips into the valleys, and emerges unbroken. We walk up and down the very steep sections, careful not to slip on the snow and ice still covering the steps. Cleverly designed watchtowers were placed two arrow shots apart. If I were an invading Mongol army, this wall would make me think twice.

The Chinese are justifiably proud of their Great Wall; it's solid evidence of a grand civilization.

· · ·

Saturday night is the loneliest night of the week according to Frank Sinatra, but I'm certain that he never spent any time in Beijing. There's no way to be lonely in the capital of the world's most populous nation. You spend most of your time dodging the masses of humanity that fill the bustling streets and sidewalks, occupying every nook and cranny of a city that seems to be bursting at the seams.

Beijing is a megacity, a place where fame and fortune draw the rich and poor alike. Fresh air, serenity, and solitude are impossible to find in this place.

I'm back at the hotel after packing three days of sightseeing into a single day and then topping off the evening with the obligatory Beijing duck dinner. (No *laowai* is allowed to exit Beijing Capital International Airport without proof of having eaten the delicious duck.)

The hotel isn't bad; it belongs to one of the international chains, a group that has properties almost everywhere in the United States as well as the big cities of the world. If I used their toll free number, I could probably book a room in Paris, Rome, or even Hattiesburg, Mississippi. It splits the difference between fancy and cheap, a predictable place in an unpredictable country.

The stores stay open late in China—no one wants to miss the opportunity to make money—so I head out for some amateur-style shopping. The women in my life laugh at my lack of shopping skills. I buy quickly, I purchase little, and I head home as soon as possible. Still, this is China, the country that invented silk, jade, $3 Rolex watches, and Chairman Mao hats, so I have to do my familial duty. This is the citadel of commerce where everything is on sale, but I turn out to be a minor blip in the Chinese economy. My purchases are few and inexpensive.

Back in the hotel lobby, I run into Michael, who is chatting with an old Beijing buddy of his named Joseph (I'm getting accustomed to these English names. If I meet a Chinese named Zhang or Li or Wang, I don't know how I'll react).

Michael urges, "John, last night in China. You must come with me and Joseph for drink. Come, we get big drink for my friend."

"I'm ready. It has been a long day, my feet are tired," I reply.

"Tired feet no problem in China. Come, we fix that."

So Michael, Joseph, and I head up to the third floor of the hotel.

We're two young Chinese men laughing, joking, full of energy, and one old American needing nothing more than to take his shoes off and rest his feet.

We are greeted at the entrance by a very attractive young woman in a cocktail dress. Next comes a rapid fire, three-way exchange. Michael, Joseph, and the woman talk non-stop. It's the unsynchronized stream of chitter and chatter I've grown accustomed to in China. Then she looks at me, smiles, and gives me a bow.

The three of us are led into a room that looks like someone's poorly decorated den. There are a couple of sofas with a coffee table in the middle, at the end of the room is a big screen television. The place is thick with cigarette smoke. None of us smoke but this room smells like it hasn't been ventilated in weeks.

Soon another attractive young woman comes in to take our orders. Michael and Joseph join her in another one of their bullet-like conversations. It sounds almost musical, the tone jumps up and down the scale. They laugh, they move their hands here and there, they sit down and then stand up. I sit there with a half-smile, wondering what's being said, searching for a pocket of fresh air.

"John, I want you to meet my friend Gloria. John is a special man, he knows all about China."

We all laugh and smile and bow.

I order my favorite Chinese beer, a Tsingtao while Michael and Joseph get some kind of cocktail. Gloria returns with the drinks and introduces two other young women, Mary and Angela.

Soon the television screen lights up, the music starts, and the microphones appear. This is karaoke, Chinese style.

I've been seeing neon signs all over China advertising KTV. The Japanese invented karaoke, but the Chinese don't like the Japanese, so in China it's not called karaoke but rather KTV. It works the same everywhere: music provided, lyrics on the video screen, you add the vocals.

Now I have to confess, I'm not a karaoke guy. In the first place, I've had very little experience. The karaoke fad came along too late to figure in my life. By the time it hit the American bar scene, I was spending my evenings changing diapers and reading bedtime stories. Sing-along on Sesame Street was probably the closest I ever came.

All my life I've been burdened with a weak, timid voice. I'm really more of a mumbler than a singer. When I try to sing loudly it sounds like I need to clear my throat. Of course, the whole vocal thing, like everything else, has gotten worse with time.

Gloria starts off with a soft Chinese ballad. She has a beautiful, melodious voice and the performance is lovely. Of course, I have no idea what she is saying; the lyrics on the screen are the usual hodgepodge of meaningless Chinese characters.

Mary and Angela follow with numbers of their own, all sung in Chinese. While one sings, the other fetches a new round of drinks. This refill service seems to function on autopilot, no questions are asked, no words are spoken, the bottles of Tsingtao continue to pile up. After a while, the bottles start to look like a phalanx of Terracotta Warriors, a formidable army of beer bottles ready to accompany me to the next world.

"John, you must sing. In China everyone sing, very important. You in China, you sing."

I beg off, with these Chinese it's important to save face. If I sing now, the game is over.

Michael takes a turn and belts out a strong forceful tune full of angst and sincerity, something like Tony Bennett would sing if he were Chinese. Joseph follows but he keeps giggling during his song, he must be a real newcomer to the KTV scene.

Next all five of my pals join together on some kind of patriotic number that sounds a lot like "Marching through Georgia." They all know the words by heart, singing and strutting in unison. They look like they are about to go on a Long March, Mao must be smiling in his mausoleum.

This is followed by a song I can handle. It's some kind of rap song. The words are in Chinese, but at the end of each verse comes the phrase in English, "Born in Beijing." I sing along, my mood improving by the minute, and at the appropriate spot in the song I yell out, "Born in Beijing." Everyone laughs and applauds, such talent in a *laowai*.

As the night rolls on, I notice that my voice is sounding better with each song. This China trip has turned out to be more fun than I could have imagined. I may have come up a little short at the 2010 IRONMAN® China, but I have enough memories to last a lifetime.

EPILOGUE

SIX IRONMAN® triathlons on six continents, all in my sixties. The time flew by fast although you'd never know it from looking at my finishing times. These days I still swim, bike, and run; it just seems to take a little longer than it used to. Sometimes I wonder how long I can keep the game going.

The memories of my trips have faded a little, but the race details are vivid, sharp, and permanent. They occupy that part of my brain formerly used for friends' names, anniversary dates, and the lyrics of old Beatles songs.

My closet holds a small fortune of IRONMAN shirts, biking jerseys, socks, jackets, caps, etc. I still place one of my IRONMAN water bottles by my pool lane when I swim. At home and at work I drink my coffee from an IRONMAN mug. I'm happy to tell anyone who's interested all about my IRONMAN travels. My accomplishments grow more impressive as each day passes.

One day I decided I should write a book about the whole experience. Now I'll have to admit there was no groundswell of public opinion demanding that my story be told. Still the whole idea made perfect sense to me. In my mind this was a triumphant tale, a modern day *Odyssey*.

Looking back, I'd always admired writers like Ernest Hemingway, James Jones, and Jack Kerouac. These men lived the bright, full life and made their rich adventures come alive in print. They're the lords of life and I could think of no good reason why I shouldn't add my name to the list.

So I've trudged along, placing myself squarely in the middle of my own story, recounting every ordeal in excruciating detail, tossing out as many anecdotes as a worn-out brain can resurrect, doing my best to make the ordinary seem extraordinary, generating heroism with a stroke of a pen.

It's been a great experience. Wandering around the world, bravely bringing up the rear in a half-dozen races, eating anything and everything placed in front of me, drinking beer with men and women of questionable repute, putting it all down on paper.

The whole thing hasn't been easy, but I've gone about as far as my energy and talents can take me . . . and I'm grateful for every minute of it.

ACKNOWLEDGMENTS

M ANY PEOPLE have helped in the writing and publishing of this book.

I want to thank Sarah Atkinson for typing the manuscript. She was with me from the very beginning when this book was just a poorly conceived idea, through the dark days when it lay unread and unnoticed, and into the hectic dash to the finish line.

Sara Priebe did a wonderful job creating the maps that help explain my travels.

I also want to thank Coop Cooper, Rob Tenery, Rick Cleveland, J.D. Simpson, and Ben Hughes for their help and advice.

I am especially thankful to Andrew Flach and Hatherleigh Press. He and Ryan Tumambing gave me the chance to see my book in print. Anna Krusinski is a very talented editor. I have greatly benefited from her skill and advice.

My children John, Eric, and Patricia have always given me love and respect and that is all a parent can reasonably ask for.

Above all I want to thank my wife, Polly. She has run the harder race but has always been there with love and support.